MARKY MARK

MARK

and the Funky Bunch

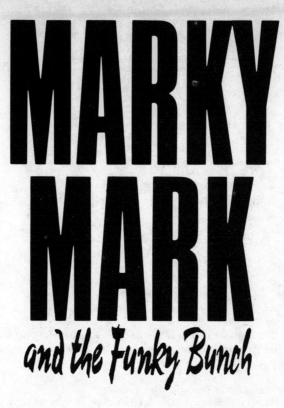

MARKY MARK

and the Funky Bunch

RANDI REISFELD

AVON BOOKS ◆ NEW YORK

MARKY MARK AND THE FUNKY BUNCH is an original publication of Avon Books. This work has never before appeared in book form.

AVON BOOKS
A division of
The Hearst Corporation
1350 Avenue of the Americas
New York, New York 10019

Library of Congress Cataloging in Publication Data:

Reisfeld, Randi
  Marky Mark and the Funky Bunch / by Randi Reisfeld.
    p. cm.
  ISBN 0-380-77100-4
  1. Marky Mark, 1971- . 2. Funky Bunch (Musical Group) 3. Rap musicians—United States—Biography.
  I. Title.
ML420.M3312R4 1992
782.42164—dc20   92-19883
[B]   CIP
                                                                   MN

First Avon Books Trade Printing: September 1992

AVON TRADEMARK REG. U.S. PAT. OFF. AND IN OTHER COUNTRIES, MARCA REGISTRADA, HECHO EN U.S.A.

Printed in the U.S.A.

ARC 10 9 8 7 6 5 4 3 2 1

Contents

MARKY MARK

and the Funky Bunch

⊙⊙⊙⊙⊙⊙⊙

The early days. "We could've taken a pretty face and made a hard-core kid... but this is me, this is my way to express myself. I will not put on a cute smile, I will not get pretty-boyed up."

Introduction

In fact, to his millions of fans spanning the globe, Marky Mark needs no introduction. He is a rapper, dancer, showman, and hip-hop hunk: simply the sexiest, most successful pop icon of the day.

Marky helped to make rap music accessible to a wide audience, without ignoring its roots in the urban ghetto, or diluting an iota of its power. He didn't need more than a single CD to get his message across, or make it count: *Music for the People* sold over one million units; Marky's first single, "Good Vibrations," shot to the number-one position on the national and international charts. His follow-up singles, "Wildside," "I Need Money," and "Peace," followed suit; his concerts are packed to the rafters with vociferous fans of all ages.

Marky's success, of course, lies beyond the hit tunes in his CD. If his message is in the music, it's just as powerfully stated—and felt—every time he takes off his shirt and drops his pants. Marky is a rock 'n' rappin' sex symbol who has his finger, and more, on the pulse of exactly what young and hip America wants to see and hear.

Though performing in the rough has become his public persona, it's really just a part of why his growing legion of fans is so hyped and so devoted. For there is more to Marky than a buff body and a talent for rap music. Beneath the macho posturing—de rigueur, after all, for rappers—beats the heart of a sensitive soul who really does care about his world and the people in it and takes every opportunity to show it.

Marky's story is heartwarming and inspiring. It is a saga of a street kid who started with nothing, who nevertheless gave up the chance of a lifetime for quick success and an easy buck, because he had to follow his heart. It is a story of family love and support, a story of two very special brothers. It is about sticking to one's beliefs against all odds.

Marky Mark and the Funky Bunch, the book, celebrates Marky—as a person *and* a cultural phenomenon.

(Chris Mackie)

A shot from the early days... before *Music for the People*, there was a publicity campaign.

1

The Baby of the Family

They say that children who come into a family after the firstborn are naturally more personable, because they are born into the ready-made comfort of a group. In Marky Mark's case, that must be true a whopping nine times over—by June 5, 1971, the day of his birth, there were eight other Wahlberg siblings making goo-goo eyes at him in the nursery. Mark Robert Wahlberg—called Marky right from the beginning—had little choice but to be sociable and doted over, for he was the last-born, the baby of the family.

Like his five brothers and three sisters before him, Marky debuted at St. Margaret's Hospital in Boston. Not surprisingly, the fair haired, hazel-eyed new baby most resembled his closest-in-age brothers Donnie and Robert (called Bobbo), for while Alma is mom to all nine kids, Donald E. Wahlberg, Sr., is proud pop to only those three. The others—Debbie, Arthur, Michelle, Paul, Jim, and Tracey—are Alma's children from two previous marriages.

Genetics, however, had less to do with keeping the 11-member clan together than close quarters, an "all for one and one for all" attitude, regular doses of religion, and surviving, for the most part, on the edge of poverty. But there was always—no matter how tough times were financially—a lot of love and a lot of laughter. They lived in a three-bedroom unit of a three-family row house on a steeply winding street in the working-class Dorchester section of Boston. When

Marky was growing up, all six boys shared a bedroom; Marky most often slept in the bunk bed below Donnie. The family pooch, Sandy, sometimes shared his bed; the turtle, named "Turtle," could usually be found in that room too. Surprisingly, it never felt crowded to Marky—sharing a room with five siblings and an assortment of pets just felt normal. He never longed for privacy. Instead, he grew up feeling secure and comfortable amid the constant clutter and camaraderie.

Of course, being in such close quarters often resulted in territorial squabbles. By Donnie's recollection, they sometimes went beyond the boundaries of broth-

The house in Dorchester where Marky grew up—his 11-member family occupied the first floor only of this three-family structure.

erly rivalry: the six boys fought almost constantly. "We were always very phys-ical with each other, there was a lot of roughhousing and some pretty bad fights," he's said. Marky wasn't spared because he was the youngest, nor would he have wanted to be. All Marky ever wanted was keep up with his big brothers, any way he could. As much as they battled between themselves—sometimes bit-terly—God forbid anyone outside the family should mess with any of them. That person would find himself up against all six boys at once. It was their own personal code of family honor, which they upheld every time.

Although Donald and Alma were strict and tried hard to limit the fighting, there was really very little they could do. After all, they weren't home all the time; they had their hands full just trying to make a living.

Donald Wahlberg supported the family as a truck driver and, later, as a bus driver who delivered prepackaged lunches to schools and summer camps. When his daily route was done, leftovers came home, for Mr. Wahlberg couldn't see good food going to waste. Donnie and Mark had the job of neatly stacking the little containers of milk in the back of the fridge and the cookies in the pantry. Sometimes the boys would deliver the food to more needy families on the block.

Like most people in their neighborhood, the Wahlbergs needed two incomes to make ends meet. So, in spite of having such a large brood to mother, Alma always worked outside the home as well. Marky remembers her working in a bank when he was quite little, and later on in a hospital. As busy and harried as she often got, however, Alma always had time for her favorite outside activity: performing. She loved to dance and though she didn't have the opportunity to pursue show business professionally, she never missed participating in the local fund-raising musicals put on at St. Gregory's Church, where the family wor-shipped. During Marky's growing-up years, he'd often troop off with his brothers and sisters to sit in the audience and applaud Mom's tap-dancing efforts onstage.

In fact, most of the entertainment Marky and his family enjoyed was home-grown. It had to be, because there was little money for extras like going to the movies, or to sports events. Instead, after Sunday dinner, there were weekly family bingo games where everyone played, including Marky's grandmother and two aunts who lived nearby. On Friday nights, the entire crew of kids would simply pile onto Mom's bed and watch TV. In the summer, on Alma's days off, she'd drive as many kids as she could stuff into the car and head for the beach.

The family took almost no vacations. The only one Marky can remember was a drive to Maine, just he, Donnie, and their parents. Camp was never an option for the kids, so most summer days were spent hanging out, playing ball among themselves and with other neighborhood kids. Marky was extremely athletic and especially talented at baseball and basketball. He, Donnie, and Bobbo spent

(Chris Mackie)

"I've faced some serious choices in my life. I usually made the wrong ones."

(Chris Mackie)

Mom Alma Conroy is proud of her baby boy—but wishes he'd keep his pants up. "I'll come home and find a new belt on my dresser," says Marky, "with a note from Mom that says, 'Please use this.'"

The street where he played as a kid was narrow, winding, and bordered on Roxbury.

almost every spring and summer eve playing ball in the park until sundown. Marky rooted for the local teams, the Red Sox, Celtics, Bruins, and Patriots, but couldn't afford to go to see them play. Instead, he'd watch TV and listen to games on the radio.

Halloween was always Marky's favorite holiday—in spite of the fact that he wasn't allowed to traipse around the neighborhood trick-or-treating. Instead, each year, his parents would set up the basement like a spook house and dress up as ghosts to "scare" the kids. There was always a big party the kids could invite friends to, and they'd bob for apples and tell ghost stories. Naturally, everyone came in costume. Marky and Donnie remember the two years in a row they dressed alike. "My sister used to take ballet classes," Marky relates, "and we'd take her tutus and dress up." Today, the family photo album has hilarious snapshots of Donnie and Marky as a pair of klutzy ballerinas.

Marky accepted early on that his family didn't have a lot of money. His clothes were hand-me-downs; he usually didn't get the toys he'd see advertised on TV. But for most of his childhood, he never really felt poor. There was always enough food and always some other family in the neighborhood that had even less. Most of his friends seemed to be pretty much in the same boat, anyway.

Besides, somehow his parents managed to come up with enough money if one of the kids really wanted something that wasn't trivial: sister Tracey got her beloved dance lessons; if the boys wanted to play Little League, sign-up money could usually be scraped up.

And there was always Christmas. And it was always a big deal. Little though he was, Marky wasn't too young to understand that his mom and dad probably saved all year to be able to buy the kids new toys for Christmas. Each Christmas morning, before the break of dawn, the nine Wahlberg kids could be found sitting on the stairs, lined up like little angels, waiting for their parents to wake up so they could rip into the presents under the tree. The year Marky remembers best was when they found nine gleaming new bicycles circling the tree. It was truly magical.

The worst time Marky can remember was the period his dad's bus company went on strike. Donald Wahlberg was a staunch union supporter and taught his brood by example to stand up for their own beliefs. He supported the strike wholeheartedly—even when his family had to go on food stamps. For the first time in his life, Marky was ashamed. "I used to be embarrassed as shit to go to the store with food stamps because all my friends would be there," he recently admitted. "I'd say, 'Dad, I don't want everybody knowin' we're on the food stamps.' Y'know what I mean?" It was a rough patch, in more ways than one, but, like his brothers and sisters, Marky came through it feeling proud of his old man, and with the eventual understanding that being poor is nothing to be ashamed of.

When he was six years old, Marky started school. Like the long line of siblings before him—Jimbo, Bobbo, Tracey, and Donnie—he too was bussed to the William Monroe Trotter School in the next neighborhood over, Roxbury, a predominately black section of town. It was on the bus going to school that Mark's brother Donnie first met Danny Wood, with whom he'd start a lifelong friendship. Mark's earliest bus and school friends were Danny's younger brother Brett Wood—and a chubby-cheeked tyke named Jordan Knight, who was his age exactly and, like Mark, the youngest in a big family. Jordan rode the bus with *his* older brother Jonathan—the two of them, of course, would one day join Donnie and Danny as the core of New Kids on the Block. But nobody knew that back in the 70s when they were all elementary-school kids. They *do* remember their friendships, though. Jordan says, "Everyone thinks I was close to Donnie when we were younger, but that isn't true. Donnie used to bully me—in a good-natured way. He'd come over and squeeze my cheeks and say, 'Jordan, you are so-o-o-o cute.' It was Mark I was close to, we were good friends and we used to hang out." Mark adds, "Me and Jordan were in the same class, second, third, and fourth grade. I'll never forget how he and Jonathan used to fight on the bus!"

Marky and Jordan may have shared the same classroom, but when the kids went to chorus, they parted ways. That's because the Knight brothers, and Danny Wood, made Mrs. Rose Holland's Trotter School chorus, while Donnie *and* Marky tried out, but never got in. At the time, it didn't really bother the Wahlberg brothers; later, they'd look back upon the whole story and laugh about it.

Of all his siblings, Marky always felt closest to Donnie, something acknowledged by their mom. "My two youngest boys were always the closest. They were constant playmates, and sometimes wrestling partners." About their fight, Marky recounts, "We had nicknames during our fights. I was always 'the crusher,' and he was 'Ling Choy,' the karate expert."

More often than fighting, however, Marky spent most of his time trying to keep up with Donnie—which was sort of a family pattern anyway. As Donnie remembers, "Me and Bobbo fought a lot and me and Mark fought a lot, 'cause we were right in that close age bracket. I wanted to show Bobbo that I was tough and old enough to hang with him and his friends, and Mark wanted to show me that *he* could hang with me and my friends. But the truth is, none of us could really hang. I couldn't deal with Bobbo and Mark couldn't deal with me."

Ah, but how Mark wanted to. "Dealing" with Donnie, in fact, must have been frustrating for Mark, for in so many ways, and even among nine kids, Donnie was a shining star. Way before New Kids, Donnie had a special magnetism; he was the kind of kid people were instinctively drawn to. Donnie *wanted* to be the center of attention—or, as he put it, "I didn't have show-*biz* aspirations, I had show-*off* aspirations"—and he usually was. Donnie was the spark plug, the one who could make everyone laugh, the born entertainer—jokey, warm, and wild. He was also the peacemaker of the family. Donnie didn't like to see anybody stay angry; he'd do everything in his power to make peace. Although Alma didn't play favorites, after her divorce it was Donnie she often turned to, "He was my

Right from the start, Marky had the dream; Donnie had the vision. Together, they would make it real.

(Chris Mackie)

protector," she's said. Furthermore, Donnie was good in school; he always had a huge posse of friends, and was rarely without a girlfriend.

Donnie was a hard act to follow.

It's not as if Donnie *tried* to overshadow Mark, but he must have. Always, Donnie felt responsible for his younger brother and tried to bolster his ego and include him in his adventures. Mark felt appreciative of Donnie's efforts—which made it all the more remarkable and hard to fathom when Marky, all on his own, one day made a decision to break away from Donnie. That decision would change the course of his entire life.

2

New Kids on the Block—Not!

When Marky was 13 years old, he walked away from the chance of a lifetime. Everyone said so, said he was crazy in the head, that he could've made a fortune, could've been a star. For a long time, it seemed that everyone was right. For in the summer of 1984, Marky and Donnie were the core of a new pop group, masterminded by a musical genius with a proven track record. They were told that the group was going to be the biggest thing the world had ever seen. They were told they were going to be rich and famous. Donnie believed it; even Alma believed it. Marky may have believed it too, but in the winter of 1984—six months after he'd joined, Marky quit.

The history of New Kids on the Block, and Marky's part in it, has been told by Mary Alford, the Boston talent manager whose concept it was originally; it's been told by Maurice Starr, the pop svengali who got the group rolling; it's been told by Alma Wahlberg, who witnessed it firsthand, and of course by her sons, Donnie and Marky.

It goes like this.

Mary Alford was a music manager on the Boston scene whose most famous client, for a short time, was Rick James. She got the idea to put together—to invent—a singing group of young boys who might rival the old Jackson 5, or the

Osmonds, so successful in the 70s. She'd already started holding auditions when, in a parking lot in Boston, she ran into Maurice Starr. Maurice had a long list of musical credentials: as a singer who'd put out albums with his brothers, as a manager, and as a producer whose latest claim to fame was the New Edition. Boston's most successful young group to date, New Edition was comprised of Bobby Brown, Johnny Gill, and the group that is now Bell Biv DeVoe. They were loaded with talent and extremely successful; unfortunately for Maurice, by 1984, they were involved in serious litigation with him, and had cut ties altogether. Maurice felt pretty burned. He, too, was looking to start from scratch and put together a new group.

Mary's recollection of their meeting: "I said to Maurice, 'I'm trying to put together a group of five young guys, like New Edition, but on the pop scene versus the R and B scene.' And Maurice said, 'you wouldn't believe it, I'm trying to do the same thing.' "

They decided to pool their efforts.

Donnie Wahlberg had become, in the meantime, a big Michael Jackson fan given to doing impromptu impressions of the star. Donnie had put together a makeshift Michael costume—including a jacket and one glove—and although he didn't really *sing*, he could rap, moonwalk, and dance just like Michael. After a while, he'd been persuaded by friends to enter talent contests, doing his Michael impressions. That's where he was seen by a girl named Gina—Mary Alford's next-door neighbor.

When Mary mentioned to Gina that she was holding open auditions, Gina said, "Oh, you've *got* to audition this kid named Donnie. He raps and he dances and he is so terrific." Problem was, Donnie was hard to find—he was not responding to any of the flyers and notices Mary had posted around town. Eventually someone told Mary that Donnie often hung out at Dorchester Park, which was right across the street from her house. Although she never found him in the park, she did find other kids who gave her his address. And one fine summer morning, she simply showed up at his doorstep.

Donnie happened to be outside when Mary came up and introduced herself, told him about the idea for a new group and asked him to audition for her and Maurice Starr. Donnie told her he had to mow the lawn—and to come back later!

Donnie recalls, "She did come back. She came back to take me to Maurice's for the audition. I went with Mark." Mary hadn't asked for Mark to come along— but between Mary's first and second visit, Donnie and Mark had made a pact: "He wasn't going if I wasn't going," was how Mark remembers it. It may simply

Donnie on Marky: "He doesn't take himself too seriously, to a point where he's like, 'I want to be a star.' He just wants to have fun, make a record."

(Craig Skinner/Celebrity Photo)

have been a case of Donnie being too scared to go on his own, but that's doubtful. There was little that frightened Donnie Wahlberg. More likely, Donnie just wanted to include his younger brother in anything that might be goin' on. Donnie always made it his business to look out for Marky.

In fact, Donnie didn't really think either one would do very well at these auditions. He was a born entertainer and leader—but he didn't really *sing*. He danced and he rapped. And Mark was starting also.

But it turned out that Maurice and Mary weren't necessarily looking for great singers. "If an incredible singer had walked through the door, a really great singer, I don't think he'd have had any better chance than I did of making the group," is Donnie's assessment. He was probably right. For it was Donnie's exuberant personality, his dancing ability, his leadership, and most of all, his magnetism that attracted Maurice's interest. Donnie was the first to make the group. As for Marky, Alma feels it was his looks that got *him* in. "They loved Mark," she has said. "They just loved him. He was little and cute." At first Mark was agreeable and went along with the program.

"Back then," Donnie says, "we were the group. Me and my little brother *were* New Kids on the Block." Maurice immediately started working with the boys, while Mary continued to scout for members. Donnie and Mark went to singing classes—given by Maurice's brothers—and began going into Maurice's home studio to start to record. "We even wrote a song together," Donnie recalls, "a rap song, a whole song, just me and Mark." That was the part Mark liked best: "Me and Donnie wrote this rap and it was so cool. It was really what I was into at the time. But then it started to turn around a bit, and Maurice would say, 'Okay, that's fine, now I want you guys to sing this ballad.'" That's when Marky began to have second thoughts about the whole deal.

For her part, Mary Alford wasn't having much success finding kids who wanted to try out; those who did didn't have the right stuff. Eventually, Donnie and Marky were asked if *they* knew of anyone . . . ? Turned out they did. They had a talented friend named Jamie Kelly, who they recruited into the group. Then they remembered their crew from the Trotter bus and chorus and got hold of Danny Wood and the Knight brothers, Jonathan and Jordan—all of whom, of course, were signed up.

As the months progressed, Marky's doubts about the whole thing began to grow stronger. "I was feeling like I just didn't fit," he acknowledged. "They were starting to do more ballady stuff, and I just couldn't see myself singing 'I'll Be Loving You Forever.'" Marky told Mary, Maurice, and Donnie that he wanted out. No one was really in favor of his decision, but they all respected it.

Marky on Donnie: "My brother understood, when no one else did. He knew I didn't like the New Kids' musical direction..."

(Chris Mackie)

(Chris Mackie)

◉◉◉◉◉◉◉◉

"Joe McIntyre is the New Kid I know the least well."

(Paul Lydon/LGI)

◉◉◉◉◉◉◉

"Some of the things New Kids has accomplished are remarkable and I give them all the respect. But when I'm asked if I'm ever rejoining, well I can't see myself rapping with Jordan Knight!"

The truth is, back then, there was no media coverage of New Kids on the Block (in fact, their original name, when Marky was still in it, was Nynuk). It's only recently that he is being asked—again and again—*why* he left New Kids. And the spin that Marky has put on that answer, that he just really wasn't into the music, that he only wanted to rap, that making the music he loved was more important than making money, doesn't quite tell the whole story. It may be *true* but at 13 years old, Marky wasn't all *that* into rap: he was more into hanging out with his friends and playing basketball and less into working. That has as much to do with why he left New Kids than a devotion to rap music. His mom has said this: "I don't think Marky knew what he wanted for a while. He did dance, and he did some rap, but he wasn't really into it. He certainly wasn't as regimented as Donnie. He was more sports-oriented and kind of lackadaisical. While it was fun, it was OK, but when it got to be hard work, he left."

In a candid moment, Mark agreed with his mother. "I don't really sing, and I was 13 and didn't want to be cooped up in a studio. I felt the group was taking up far too much of my time. I was young and I just wanted to be a kid."

Whatever Donnie may have really felt about Mark's decision at that moment, his on-the-record comment is this: "I respect him for not staying with the group. It took a lot for him to stand up and say, 'No, this is not what I want to do.' Because everyone was pressuring him to stay with it, telling him, 'You'll be rich, you'll do this, you'll do that, you'll be famous.' So for him to stand up and say no, that took a lot of strength and a lot of character, and I respect him for it. I hope he doesn't have any regrets."

Marky doesn't own up to many. Beyond an occasional twinge of envy, he insists, "Hey, I'm happy. I didn't miss out. I did what I wanted to, and I'm content. I have no regrets."

When the group's very first, self-titled album came out, there wasn't much for him to regret. The boys—minus Jamie Kelly, but plus Joe McIntyre—had worked long, hard hours, only to have a major flop on their hands. The record went nowhere; the single, "Be My Girl" is hardly a footnote in their history.

3

The Wild Child

Marky had never been the world's most obedient child. The straight and narrow was not a path he could ever find, much less follow. According to his, and even Donnie's, own admission pushing the edge of the envelope, testing the limits—at home, school, and on the street—just came naturally. "We was just these wild kids, the type who wanted to try things," Donnie has attempted by way of explanation. Mark was that in spades.

Childish pranks were part of his everyday life. At 12—and no doubt against his parents' wishes—he decided to give himself a tattoo. He drew a picture of a "a shamrock thing" on his left leg; using unsterilized sewing needles and a bottle of India ink, he made the design permanent. It was a painful procedure. Now, Marky admits it was "a stupid kid thing to do"; it looked so ridiculous that he eventualy covered it up with a professional job. But back then, he thought it made him look tough and macho. Besides, he equated enduring pain with measuring up as a man. He felt, at times, impervious to pain.

If he was admonished to be careful, that was Marky's cue to find the most dangerous way out of any situation. He's got the bruises to prove it, and even today, he still talks the tough-boy talk. "I got bruises and scars all over my body," he says with bravado. "I got one on the inside of my knee from falling

(Albert Ferreira/DMI)

"Donnie *is* wild, but it's not like he's trying to be . . .
That's just the way he is. That's how he grew up."

through a fire escape on the fifth floor—the stair was missing. I got scars all over just from bein' a wild little kid."

Scarred, but never scared—not then and not now. As he told a British journalist, "I ain't scared of nothin'. Not death, not spiders, nothin'. I'm not the kind of guy that gets freaked out."

He was, however, the kind of guy who dropped out. One of the traits that differentiated Marky from Donnie was his reaction to school. While neither could be called an academic superstar, Donnie at least was a good student. His grades throughout elementary and middle school were better than average. Things came easily to Donnie. He was popular, his teachers liked him, he is fondly remembered. Marky had a more difficult time of it, all the way through and on every level: social, academic, disciplinary.

After completing sixth grade at the Trotter School, Marky was enrolled in the Phyllis Wheatley Middle School, and then Copley High, just like most of his brothers and sisters before him. He remembers frequently being recognized by the teachers: *Oh, yeah, you're another of those Wahlberg kids.* He does not remember any of it with fondness. "I hated it. With a passion. I hate that shit. I made trouble...I made my protest through not being there."

Which turns out to be quite an understatement. Especially as he started high school, Marky wasn't there a lot more often than he was. "I swear I left home every day *meaning* to go to school...but I'd meet my posse in front, hang out, and then walk off, hit the stores. I was always down at the mall, hangin' out down the street or at the local pizza joint."

Marky insists it was his spotty attendance record—which no doubt contributed to his lackluster grades—that dealt him what had to be the most humiliating blow of his young life: he got left back in ninth grade. Which came first, the chicken or the egg: did Marky really skip school because he couldn't compete academically, or did he do poorly because he cut most of the time? Marky feels it was the latter. "It wasn't that I was dumb, I just felt there was better stuff on the streets." Whichever the root of the problem, one obviously exacerbated the other. The result? Marky was a failure at school. The objective of making children repeat a grade is so they'll learn what they missed. In Marky's case it didn't work. His response to the humiliation of being left back was to be even more truant. "I went to school maybe 10 times [that next year]. I kept hooking off all the time." Which couldn't possibly lead anywhere else but exactly where it did: Marky officially dropped out of school in tenth grade.

And once he was on the streets full time, trouble was around every corner. Although Marky himself has not gone into great detail about his early life of crime, he has owned up to some of it: scamming for change, underage drinking, and shoplifting (or "doing runs," as Marky has termed it). In weak defense, Marky once told a British journalist, "Our family was very big, so we didn't have much money at all. I started stealing stuff...if I saw something in a shop that I couldn't afford, I'd just try and steal it anyway."

Petty crimes led to more serious offenses. Marky totals up his arrest record at "five or six, but only two as an adult." Since Marky had the tendency to use his fists more often than his brains, both adult arrests were for assault and battery—luckily, all charges, in both incidents, ended up being dismissed.

The truth is that Marky was not in a place where luck was going to come into play very often. He was in his late teens and at that point the main "rap" in his life was on rap sheets. He looked like a kid headed for the slammer. "I was uncontrollable," he admits.

What put Marky on the path from a prank-prone, curious kid to near-felon was no doubt a combination of influences, absences, and a whole lot of self-doubt. The neighborhood he grew up in was a rough one. The Dorchester section of Boston, while boasting its share of hardworking, law-abiding families, also has its share of gangs, guns, drugs, and kids who hang out on street corners with nothing much to do but get into trouble. All the boys who became New Kids on the Block—save one—grew up there and tell similar tales of typical street life and petty crime: from jumping subway turnstiles to dodging bullets during gunfights. Easy money was available—and you didn't have to look too hard to find it. It was a tempting, seductive life-style, especially for a boy who wasn't finding success or any kind of fulfillment at school.

But Marky was influenced by more than people he met on the street; he found powerful ones in his own home. When he was 11, his parents divorced, which is rough on *any* kid. Although Mark's dad moved out, he was never far away, and Marky continued to see him. But the family had come unglued—even on holidays, they were no longer together. We'd have two Christmases," Donnie has detailed. "One at our mom's and then another at our dad's."

Marky was hardly the first of his family to get into trouble. A few of his brothers struggled with drug and substance abuse problems. Even Donnie had smoked and *tried* to drop out of school twice—he eventually finished up with a tutor. Brother Jimbo has an arrest record and has been in jail. He has publicly admitted his problems. In fact, a completely reformed Jimbo now lectures at schools about staying out of trouble.

But even back then and even while he was getting into all sorts of trouble, Jimbo tried to be a positive influence on Donnie and warn him away from life in the wrong lane. By all accounts, Donnie took that advice seriously. He would

"I kept hearing, 'You *can't* have a show-biz career if your big brother already has one—look at Frank Stallone, or Joey Travolta!'"

(Craig Skinner/Celebrity Photo)

have passed it on to Marky, but the sad fact was that during the years that Marky probably needed him most, Donnie was nowhere near home.

Donnie had joined New Kids in 1984, but it wasn't until '86 that he hit the road, promoting the group and their first album. In the beginning—'86 through '88—although Donnie wasn't away constantly, Marky must have felt the absences keenly, for the two had never been separated before. Starting in 1989, with the release of the New Kids' *Hangin' Tough* album, Donnie began to be away for longer and longer stretches. Home became little more than a pit stop. The physical separation led to an emotional one between the brothers. In a rare

(Gregg DeGuire/London Features)

"I never had any big plans for being a star. I just wanted to do my music, y'know?"

introspective moment, Marky admitted, "When I was growing up, Donnie was sort of a cross between a big brother and a hero to me. We were best buddies and used to hang out together all the time. When he started to spend all of his time at rehearsals, we drifted apart, and suddenly when I was 15, he was famous. I hardly saw him at all for ages. We really grew apart."

It couldn't have helped Marky's own sense of self-worth that Donnie and the New Kids—which Marky had walked away from—suddenly seemed the most popular and successful pop group on the planet. As 1990 began, each Kid was a millionaire—imagine how that must have felt for a kid from the streets who used to be embarrased about food stamps. Marky continued to insist he wasn't jealous... but that would have taken almost superhuman sensibilities.

In fact, the tidal wave that was New Kids on the Block wasn't even real to Marky at first. It wasn't until Donnie invited him to hang out on the occasional road trip that Marky understood what it all meant. For what Marky saw close up was not so much the millions, but the tangible perks: the limousines, the fancy hotel rooms, the luxury tour buses, the bodyguards, the legions of devoted fans. There was a support staff at Donnie's beck and call: there was someone to do his hair, someone to wash and press his clothes, someone to do his makeup, always someone to do his bidding. He could get, it seemed to Marky, just about anything he craved—a cheeseburger at two in the morning, the latest Nintendo game, some female companionship—at any time. All Donnie had to do was ask. The New Kids had a term for it: they called it "livin' large."

Who wouldn't be jealous of that? Especially when Marky realized that he too could have had it all. He never felt any less talented musically than his brother or the New Kids. He just hadn't wanted to be in the group at the time—but unlike Jamie Kelly, the other New Kid who'd quit before the group hit it big, Marky was face to-face with the enormity of it all. It wasn't something he could easily get away from. The upside of astounding success wasn't hard to see, or to take.

New Kids mania affected Marky's life even when he wasn't hanging out on the road with them. Fans had found his family's home, and began camping out on the front steps, hoping for a glimpse of Donnie. Alma remembers the first startling incident: "We were in bed one evening, and fans were peeking in our living-room window... They were playing New Kids music out in front of the house at 2 A.M. and calling for Donnie to come out! We've had our phone number changed three times."

The situation at home was changing in more ways than that. As Donnie was getting deeper and deeper into his life as a New Kid, so was his mom Alma. At

"All of a sudden, people get this crazy attitude when you stand up for yourself. That's all. That's my attitude."

(Chris Mackie)

first, to make sure Donnie was with people who were legitimate, Alma spent many hours scoping out the situation: later, she got caught up in the whirlwind of excitement. Alma was at many New Kids rehearsals and gigs—"here, there, and everywhere," as she remembers those early days. She even helped start the family-run New Kids fan club. All of which was thrilling, but had to take her attention somewhat away from Marky.

Another wonderful development in Alma's life that took her focus away from Marky: she got remarried, to a man named Mark Conroy. That, at least, turned out to be a positive influence in Marky's life, for Mr. Conroy never tried to take Donald Wahlberg's place, but instead became a friend to Marky.

Just as it took a combination of forces to bring Marky to the verge of jail, it took another, more powerful combination to turn his life around. The inclusion of Mark Conroy in his life was probably one of them. Another was the Dorchester Youth Collaborative. That's the place he was sent after his brushes with the law. As Marky describes it, "It's a youth center where kids like me hang out to get away from trouble. It's a great place that helps lots of kids. They just tell you, 'You screwed up. Look at your life.' "

Marky was in a place, at 19 years old, where he finally could. He took that advice seriously. "I realized that I was on the verge of ruining my life."

Realizing it and doing something about it, however, are two different things. Marky—at first by himself, and, later, with Donnie's help—did both.

4

Raised on Rap

Aside from a gift for getting into trouble, the teenage Mark Wahlberg did have one other significant talent, and that was for rap music. Since infancy, in fact, a music mix had been a constant in his life, courtesy of his family. Mom Alma always had either the radio or the stereo on. She'd relieve the drudgery of housework by dancing to the beat. Mark's older brothers Artie and Paul filled the house with their grooves of choice—hard rock and heavy metal. "They were into Led Zeppelin, AC/DC, and The Who," Marky remembers. Donnie Wahlberg has said that *his* earliest musical influences were a combination of the heavy metal he heard at home and the rap he heard on the street—but for Mark, it was rap and only rap that turned him on, right from the start. Mark claims he was a hip-hop fan by the age of four.

Maybe. But it wasn't until he was just a touch older and riding the bus to school in Roxbury that rap music was, as he says, "in my face every day." As countless kids on school and camp buses have done for generations, the children on Marky's bus filled the travel time by singing. Their songs mirrored what *they* heard at home, and because these were inner-city kids, those songs were hip-hop songs. When "Rapper's Delight" became the first commercial rap song, the kids on the bus were way into it already.

"I'm not trying to brag about the hard times and sound like I'm some big tough guy. There are a lot of people like me. I just survived the streets."

The musical medley continued at school—in the yard, in the halls, in the boys' rooms. Later on in life, when Marky (and Donnie too) would be accused of raiding rap riffs from the black community, the Wahlberg brothers needed only to look back to their elementary-school years in rebuttal. As Donnie said, "When rap music first started, if I wasn't in the school I was in, I probably *wouldn't* have been exposed to it . . . but I was in the school that I was in, and I *was* exposed to it. That's what I grew up on." Ditto for Mark.

If school was the reason Marky heard a lot of rap, Donnie was the primary reason he started writing it. For Donnie loved to write and found writing those

Who, me, a sex symbol?
"All I want to
do is make dope raps . . ."

(John Paschal/Celebrity Photo)

rhyming raps a perfect way to express himself: his very first raps were written with his little brother. "The first time I heard a rap, I wrote a rap—me and my little brother Marky. It was funny," Donnie's divulged. The second rap coproduction by the brothers was a five-page-long satire about then-President Ronald Reagan.

In those days there still wasn't a lot of rap being played on the radio, so Donnie and Marky would scour the record stores to hear more. The first rap records Marky remembers getting hold of—he won't exactly admit to shoplifting, but has been quoted as saying, "I got them for nothing, heh, heh"—were by Grandmaster Flash, Afrika Bambatta, and the more obscure Molly Moll.

It wasn't until Donnie began getting away from rap and into New Kids, however, that Mark really began to adopt it as something entirely his own. "It got to a point where I was *always* rapping," Marky says. "Even when I was a knucklehead, skipping school, I was rapping." Making up original raps seemed to come naturally—and constantly. "I was always thinking in terms of rap," Marky remembers. "Sometimes I'd rhyme about this, sometimes I'd rhyme about that. Sometimes I'd get stuck; then other times, I'd be hanging around, in a daze, and then all of a sudden, I'd come up with a rap. Half the time I didn't have a pen to write it down."

By the age of 15, he'd started to perform—in the most amateur way—as well. His earliest "performances" took place on the street corners of Dorchester, Roxbury, and neighboring Mattapan. Along with his own posse, which sometimes included Rasta Phil and the Brizia, members of today's Funky Bunch, Marky would show up on a corner with a beat box and get down to freestyle rhyming and breakdancing. The mix of teens in Marky's musical posse seemed to change daily. Prior to the Funky Bunch, Marky was in only one "official" group, which was called Electric Generation.

With or without a group, Marky progressed from impromptu street corner gigs to playing at parties, and then at local clubs. Much as he loved it, the truth is, he didn't really perform with enough consistency to develop a following, or even a reputation locally. In fact, those who were on the Boston rap and breakdance scene in those days say they don't remember him at all! He certainly didn't make any money rapping back then.

Since he wasn't in school, Marky had little choice but to get a job. During his late teen years, he worked at several and remembers a few of them well. "I was a construction worker and then I worked in a hospital. I trained to be a mechanic, lotsa things just to get by, y'know?" In reflection, however, Marky looks back on those days with a sense of pride. "Last job I had, I was a bricklayers' apprentice. And I was happy with that job, because it was something that made

"Basically, I am a street kid who is trying to do something positive with my life."

"With a smaller crowd, it's real easy to reach people. It's almost like a one-on-one confrontation, right in your face."

(Paul Lydon/LGI)

me feel good. To build a wall for the side of a building really felt good to me. It was an accomplishment. One building we rebuilt was a place I used to hang out at, and it was weird to see my name all over its walls!"

Marky's stints of manual labor during the day and freestyle rap performances at night were frequently interrupted by trips to see his brother on the road, especially during 1989 and 1990. Once he got over the shock of just how big New Kids were—and just how much he'd given up—Marky began to get a feel for what life as performer was really like. From the wings, he'd not only see fans clamoring for Donnie, some of them even started to ask for *him* by name. For

(Paul Lydon/LGI)

"In my show, I come out more powerfully on the lyric end of things, just to let them know what I'm about, straight from the get-go."

Donnie had given many interviews by that time and *always* talked about his younger brother. By association, Marky got a tiny taste of fame. It tasted good.

Even better, however, was the taste of professional performing allowed to him by Donnie. Way before the Funky Bunch, Donnie had invited Marky to take part in the New Kids Coca-Cola commercial in 1990 and gave him brief parts in the "Step by Step" and "Games" videos.

A funny thing happened to Marky after those experiences. It struck him that he truly wasn't jealous of Donnie, that for whatever reasons, he *had* made the right decision all along way back then. He *didn't* really care all that much about

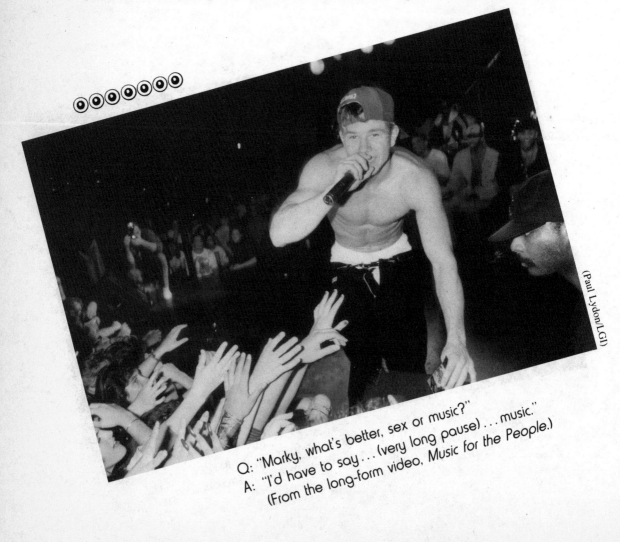

(Paul Lydom/LGI)

Q: "Marky, what's better, sex or music?"
A: "I'd have to say . . . (very long pause) . . . music."
(From the long-form video, *Music for the People*.)

Making the understatement of the year.

the fame and fortune, but, whadya know, he *did* love to perform. Back at the Dorchester Youth Collaborative, Marky had realized that he was on the verge of ruining his life. But it wasn't until the middle of 1990 that he knew what he was going to do about it. At that point, he made his second most important decision. He was going to become a professional rapper, do whatever he had to, work as hard as he had to, go for it with everything that was in him.

He also knew exactly how he would make that happen.

5

The Dream

Truth is, the dream really began with Donnie. In fact, Donnie had begun planning for Mark's solo rap career long before Mark got serious, and long before anything would come to fruition. As Donnie tells it today, back when Mark left New Kids, a brotherly promise had been made between the two—albeit an unspoken one—that if the Kids ever made it to the big time, Donnie would come back and help Mark achieve whatever his goal was. He knew it might take a while, but felt, "If I could help him get his vision out someday, I'd do it."

From time to time the brothers talked about working together, but only in the vaguest "Yeah, that'd be cool, we'll get to it someday" kind of way—and never at length. Mark recollects, "We'd talk about it for a while, but we were never really serious, 'cause there never was any time to do anything together." Donnie was *always* on the road, in the studio, at a photo shoot, on the west coast, or New York doing business.

But every once in a while during a phone call home, Donnie would suggest to Mark that he start putting some of his freestyle raps to music. He suggested it with increasing frequency, but it wasn't until Donnie got to take some extended time off the road that he and Mark *did* start writing some rough raps together. Those first few attempts, they recall with a laugh, were kind of down and dirty. "We did a nasty version of the Commodores' 'Brickhouse' and an original, called

(Paul Lydon/LGI)

"If my fans listen to my music, then they're gonna know what I'm about."

'Baby, Bring Home the Bacon.' We just kept coming up with more raps and every song was better than the last," said Donnie.

The brothers were really getting down with the music, but just as they'd get cooking, Donnie inevitably was called back to work. And with Donnie away, Mark inevitably went back to play.

And then, somewhere between gigs in Augusta, Georgia, and Chapel Hill, North Carolina, on one of those long, lonely, all-night bus trips, Donnie was suddenly hit with a lightning bolt of inspiration. It was early March of 1990 and he just *knew* that it was time to get serious about Marky. It was time for Marky to launch a professional career as a rapper. And it was time for Donnie to get behind it.

The more he thought about it, the more turned on he got. As he giddily confided in those wee hours one morn, "My little brother's project, that's gonna be my favorite one. It's gonna be challenging for me and we're both gonna enjoy it. I think we'll *both* get a lot out of it. He wants to have fun and try it, see what would really happen if he stuck with this. And I have a lot of stuff I want to do musically I'm gonna get to really do a lot, put a lot of *me* into that."

Donnie's need to prove to himself, and to the world, that he could do more than be a New Kid on the Block, was powerful. As much as he loved and appreciated being part of the group, he wasn't fulfilled artistically. Donnie wanted to write music—something the Kids didn't do at all on their first three albums—and he wanted to produce and he wanted to rap. New Kids, in fact, hadn't begun to tap Donnie's talent. As a result, Donnie dabbled in other musical projects. He'd already gotten behind a couple of new Boston bands and by March 1990 was in full swing writing and producing for what seemed at the time the most promising of them, a rap trio called the Northside Posse.

When Donnie realized that it was time to work with his own blood brother seriously, he phoned home and got Marky on the line. "Yo, I'm busy writing all these songs for other people. Mark, it's time. I'm gonna do one for you." Donnie's timing was dead on. It coincided exactly with Marky's own realization that rap was going to be his life. As Mark put it, "We just decided, 'All right, it's time. Let's do it.' " Once the Wahlberg boys were in sync, there was no stopping this train.

Donnie started the engine by making the first most important decision about Marky's record. *He* would produce it. Along with Mark, he'd cowrite it. And, most crucial of all, *he* would finance it. Donnie was going to be in complete control, much the same way, perhaps, as Maurice Starr had been in complete musical control of the New Kids projects.

◉◉◉◉◉◉◉

"I'm doing this my way...without hiding myself.
That's how I am."

Donnie's decision was not based on his need to be a control freak. He just felt, for starters, that he knew his brother better than anyone. "Mark is very real and very raw... personally and musically, he's very straightforward," Donnie detailed. Further, Donnie had the skills to put a musical machine together, he knew who to hire to get the job done. He certainly had the financial resources. It made good sense for Donnie to be the man in charge.

Marky and Donnie, working together at last, visualized the entire mix. The concept was to present Marky, the rapper and dancer, fronting a hot group, which would include a deejay, male and female dancers, *and* a live band, the last of which is unusual for rappers. Backing it all up would be the most slammin' original rap riffs anyone had ever heard. There was even a name Donnie had been diddling with: Marky Mark and the Funky Bunch.

Making Marky Mark and the Funky Bunch a reality was going to take a lot of work and a lot of time. Donnie was ready, and Marky was there, fully committed and balls-on serious. So when Donnie would bolt awake in the middle of the night with a flash of inspiration and call Marky in at 4:00 A.M. to lay down some tracks, Marky was up for it. In fact, during the entire period that the songs were written and recorded and the act was being put together, Marky was more than willing to take a lot of guidance. Donnie had put in *his* years learning the ropes; Marky knew it was his turn to do the same.

One of the people Donnie had learned from, so many years back, was music manager Mary Alford. Though a central figure in New Kids' genesis, Mary had taken a backseat once the group began to really roll. The perception that Maurice Starr was the only genius behind the group was pervasive. But it never had been completely true. Donnie had not forgotten Mary's vital contributions. He also knew her dedication and the depth of her knowledge and talent. It was very possibly a combination of wanting to make amends to Mary (or "M-Lou," for "Mary-Lou," as he and Marky affectionately call her) and simply knowing that she'd do the best job for his brother *and* that he could trust her that led Donnie to bring her into Marky's mix right from the start.

Donnie approached Mary with the idea in New York, in 1990. His enthusiasm was infectious. Mary, who'd of course known Mark for all those years, caught on immediately and was quick to jump in. She became Marky's interim manager and, back in Boston, started to put it all together. Working with Donnie and Marky, she auditioned potential Funky Bunchers: it was Mary who found Terry Yancey, the man who became Marky's deejay, and she who found several of the other backup dancers and band members.

The actual recording was done not only in studios around Boston and New England, but sometimes—just as the New Kids had done with Maurice—catch-as-catch-can, on the road. "We did a lot of stuff in hotel rooms," Marky said. "Only thing we wouldn't do in the hotel room was record vocals. We would go to a local 24-track studio for that. We did one song in Kansas, one in Arkansas, and one in St. Louis." That part of the process was admittedly hectic, but Marky loved it. "It can be fun, too, y'know?"

Slowly, throughout the process, a more confident Marky was starting to emerge. Certainly, he took direction from Donnie, Mary, and those with more experience who knew the score. But with each step along the way, he began to feel a little more confident and secure.

There were the lengthy discussions about the music itself, which songs and what kind of songs, would end up on the album. Straight up, Donnie, Marky, and Mary knew that if they went ahead and just did a pure rap album, there would be a backlash. There were sincere concerns about how the black community would react to a white rapper—and also how Marky's potential fans, all those little girls who loved New Kids and were prepared to love Marky, would react to a hard-core rap album. Marky breaks down their thinking: "The choice was, should I *not* do what I want to do for fear of reaction, *or* should I do it and be honest?" Marky, of course has always believed that his rapping *is* as honest and true as anyone's, regardless of skin color. He declares, "Some people grew up on rhythm 'n' blues. Some people grew up on rock 'n' roll. Hip-hop's been around since I was four. That's what I listened to. *I'm* part of the hip-hop culture."

With that, the choice was made. "I just decided to be true to myself," Marky says. He hoped that the fans would understand. But he felt that even if they didn't, and if, without their support, *he* didn't become as rich or as famous as his brother, well, that would be just fine. For this is how Marky really feels. "There's nothing like rapping at a local club like the Gallery in Dorchester with 30 people in the place who know what it's about—not 70,000 young girls who don't truly understand hip-hop music. I'm not putting them down, but if they're going to listen to rap, they should know the roots of the music, where it's coming from. I make a dope rap. If I can make the guys on the corner bob their heads with my lines, I could be barefoot, but my whole day is saved."

Marky made his choice realizing full well that the street flavor of the album he was putting together was "gonna come as shock to some people, but that's how I am. My music is about more than making money, or else I wouldn't put so much into it, or as much meaning. I already get fan mail, but if I cater to just that audience with all dance songs, I wouldn't be true to myself and be able to express my own feelings."

Marky also decided right off not to worry about that other brick sure to be thrown at him: the one labeled nepotism, that said he only got to make an album because of who his brother is, and that very likely, he'd just come out riding Donnie's musical coattails. Marky was prepared. "What else are people gonna think until they hear the music?" he asked rhetorically. "They say, 'Donnie's brother is coming out with a record.' Basically, what they're expecting is to see the same old thing. Or if they knew it was going to be a rap album, they'd probably think it was gonna be something like Vanilla Ice, or Hammer. Why would anyone think that a 20-year-old kid could come out really *saying* some-

"I'm proud that I got the chance to be in this position, but I won't do anything that feels uncomfortable."

(Janet Macoska)

Winning awards: "Success is the icing on the cake."

(John Paschal/Celebrity Photo)

thing? Besides, [being Donnie's brother] can only help me. I'm not depending on it to carry me, but it can help me in the door."

But it only cracked the door. Having his record cowritten, financed, and produced by New Kid Donnie wasn't all that much of a shortcut to success. Although Donnie had bragged, "Oh, yeah, I'll have him signed to a record label, no problem," truth is, it took a bit longer than originally anticipated. And they had to go through the same process as any other newcomer. "We recorded demo tapes and sent them out to record labels, just like anyone else," Donnie admitted. The demo consisted of three original songs. One of the people they sent it to was Mark Benesch, once a major player at Columbia Records (the New Kids' label), now head of promotion at Interscope Records, part of the giant Warner/Elektra/Atlantic conglomerate. He loved the demo and passed it on to Jimmy Iovine, president of the label, who reportedly flipped over "Good Vibrations."

Although other labels expressed interest, Interscope offered Marky Mark and the Funky Bunch the best deal. They believed in Marky, shared the vision and the dream. When the time was right, they put their marketing muscle where their mouths were.

Meantime, the entire crew was working furiously to finish up the album, rehearse, and get a show together. Part of the plan was to have it all ready to go by the end of 1991, so Marky Mark and the Funky Bunch could get their first official taste of performing. The hope was to have them open in Europe for the New Kids. Which would let the baby band get the on-stage experience it needed and test out the material, all wrapped in a kind of security blanket, with a very "paternal" figure—namely Donnie—hovering protectively in the wings.

6

Music for the People

The debut album by Marky Mark and the Funky Bunch was unleashed on an unsuspecting public on July 23, 1991, one and a half years from its conception. The brothers called it *Music for the People*, which they felt said it all. "Not for the money or the fame or the sequel, I make music for the goddamn people!" Those lyrics, from the title song, explained Marky's purpose: he didn't make the album to cash in on Donnie's success, didn't care if it made a dime. He just wanted to express himself and put something out there for *his* people, the people of the streets.

"The record speaks for itself," Marky declared upon its release. "I had a lot to say. I thought it would do some good and I thought people like myself could relate to it. I know a lot of people like myself."

Well, whadya know, the people—and not only those who, like Marky, grew up poor—liked what they heard. While some may have expected a G-rated New Kids clone, they welcomed with open arms (and open wallets) the very "rated R"—for real, raw, and rough—record that Marky put out.

"The record is very versatile," he explained. "It has a very serious side to it—a lot of strong statements—and it has a fun side, a lot of dance tunes. I want people to take a positive message from it, but also be entertained by it. I want to make people dance and have a good time."

"We're like a family, y'know what I'm sayin'?" Funky Bunch members (left to right): Terry, Mark, Hector, Ashey, Scottie.

(Robin Kennedy/London Features)

Lyrically, *Music for the People* covered the territory Marky knew best, tackling themes of racial tension and acknowledging, but decrying, the drugs and violence of the streets he grew up on. Musically, Marky took on only one theme: white boys can rap too. For *Music for the People* is, above everything else, a down 'n' dirty, in-your-face, slammin', street-smart hip-hop album. Marky and Donnie wouldn't have had it any other way.

Behind the controls, *Music for the People* was a family affair. The entire album, of course, was produced under the umbrella of Donnie D. Productions. Beyond brother Donnie's obvious and ubiquitous participation—including production, arrangements, writing, backup vocals, and laying down a few solo raps—many others in the New Kids/Boston family lent their talents as well. Maurice Starr, along with a couple of his musical siblings, contributed to several tunes; Danny Wood wrote and produced one; Jordan Knight lent his mellifluous tones to another. Friends of the extended New Kids clan climbed aboard too. MC Spice, a legendary Boston rapper, and deejay Terry Yancey, both brought into the fold by Mary Alford, rounded out the crew on the record.

Partly recorded and mostly mixed at Newbury Sound Studios in Massachusetts, the record itself had a big sound featuring live guitar and bass instead of the routine drum beats and bass lines most rap recordings employ. Which made it kinda fun to dance to, as well as listen and learn from.

Divided into "Wild Side" and "Smoove Side," Marky's record runs roughshod over eleven electrifying tracks. He comes out swinging on the first one, the title tune "Music for the People." Written by the Wahlberg bros, it not only lays down the record's concept, but jumps right into rap's sampling controversy head on.

Most rap songs borrow music and lyrics from the records of other artists. They simply play an excerpt from another record and plant it in between their own rap verses. The most famous examples are Hammer's "You Can't Touch This," which sampled verses from Rick James' "Superfreak," and Vanilla Ice's "Ice, Ice, Baby," which featured the Queen/David Bowie song "Under Pressure." While the rap community calls this process sampling (and say it's indigenous to the art form), some of the artists who've been sampled *from* have another word for it. *They* call it stealing. The main objection was that (until recently) rappers rarely credited the original musicians, let alone compensated them financially.

Marky had his own take on the situation, explained in "Music for the People." In his lyrical view, he's only helping the original artists—who should be happy, even *grateful*, for the new exposure. "I make an old song dope again, give a played-out pop star hope again," is what Marky wrote. Marky put his money where his mouth is: at each turn, he credited the original songwriter and paid royalties.

Sampling isn't the only issue Marky tackles on the title tune. He disputes the notion that as a white rapper, he's stealing from the black community; he disses the Vanilla Ice comparisons (that's a sore point with Marky); says he doesn't care what the critics think and hardly expects a Grammy for his efforts. His music, he concludes, is for *everyone*: white, black, Russian, German, Jewish, Puerto Rican, Portuguese . . . the world!

"Good Vibrations," the second song on the album, was chosen as the first single. That proved a wise decision, for the infectious loosey-goosey dance tune—with powerful vocals by Loleatta Holloway—was an instant smash. As Mark himself joked, "It's a track that could make George Bush move!" But in between the feel-good verses and sample of "Love Sensation," Marky managed a message: "I'm anti D-R-U-G-G-I-E, my body is healthy . . . " The people got the message and felt those vibrations all right—the record went to number one on the pop charts.

Marky packed his most powerful political punch on "Wildside," a no-holds-barred condemnation of drug abuse, racism, murder, and gang violence. The lyrics depict people who made the wrong choices, and didn't live to tell about it. Based on (and heavily sampled from) Lou Reed's "A Walk on the Wildside," Marky's version is updated, R-rated, and revised. While the original observed and appreciated those who choose to live on the edge, Marky's version warns of the dangers. He explains, "The story I'm tellin' . . . is all about things that happened in and around Boston, very serious things that I thought were important for me to speak about. Like racial tension in the Boston area. It's a very serious issue."

To the first verses—which poignantly picture good people led astray—Marky adds the two new verses about real-life crimes that made shocking headlines on his own mean streets. One is about Charles Stuart, a man "who had everything going for him," but murdered his wife and tried to pin the crime on a black man. That Charles' dastardly deeds resulted in his own suicide, Marky says, "That's how it is on the wildside!" The last verse mourns for "Little Tiffany, only thirteen," who was the victim of a random drive-by shooting. She's immortalized in Marky's song, not as someone who chose life in the fast lane, but as an "innocent," caught up and mowed down, by just being close to the wildside.

Lest anyone get the impression that Marky is all politics and preaching, " 'Bout Time I Funk You" is a slam-bam reminder that boy rappers like to brag about

"Different things inspire me, different places. I get ideas for songs driving down the street, or riding on the bus."

(Janet Gough/Celebrity Photo)

what's on their minds . . . namely, girls and sex. Written by Donnie and Marky, with help from Maurice Starr and backup vocals by Donnie and Jordan Knight, this track pretty much lays it on the line right in the title. Hint: it has little to do with romance. It could, of course, be about *music* . . . but anyone over 16 who reads the lyrics probably has another interpretation. 'Nuff said.

"Peace" could be subtitled "Everybody rap now!" as this is the track where Marky gives some of his homeboys a chance at a verse. Contributions come from Donnie (he's the one referred to as Cheeze—it's his longtime nickname), the Boston rap groups Def Duo and the Northside Boys, MC Spice, and Marky

(Marko Shark/LGI)

"I'm not sayin' that I'm this squeaky-clean little kid, y'know what I'm sayin'? I never said that."

himself. Though each got the shot at an original rap, all the verses are tied together with the salutation "Peace."

"So What Chu Sayin' " ends the first side with Marky copping a major 'tude (attitude): once again, our boy comes out swinging as he returns to one of his recurrent themes: the criticism that rap music is a black art form and whites who do it are not only phonies, but thieves. Marky opens with song with the brazen acknowledgment, "All right, all right, here's another MC whose skin is white..." and goes on from there. He drops the names of other white rappers and admits, "When white boys rap, the public sees it as just a novelty. But anybody can do rap if you stay true to the art form and are not trying to take anything away from it." Still, Marky lays claim to some major differences between himself and the others. He goes back to his hip–hop roots, saying, "I do hip-hop from the heart, so don't label me a phony or a sellout." More importantly, he gives respect to the "old school," those who created this form of music.

Smoove Side begins with "Marky Mark Is Here," a standard-issue I'm-the-best-and-I'm-gonna-out-rap-anybody-in-the-room groove that appears in some form or another on most rap records. It's more than just bragging though. Songs like this have their roots in street-corner rap competitions. And in Marky's tune, he once again tips his lyrical hat to the (black) "pioneers who shed tears for years ... I give much respect, won't ever forget...."

"On the House Tip," written by Donnie and Spice, is indeed a house anthem (dance-club tune). On this one, Marky gives the floor to his Funky Bunch, each of whom get to make their mamas proud by doing a solo verse. Ashey Ace (Andy Thomas), Scotty G. (Scott Ross), DJ T (Terry Yancey), and Hector-the-Booty-Inspector (Hector Barrows) introduce and express themselves in their own in-imitable manner.

Beats there the heart of a real romantic beneath Marky's tough-guy macho pose? "Make Me Say Ooh!" could make one say, "Maybe." For this track has the real distinction of being the one sweet, romantic rap on the record. Marky gets lovey-dovey addressing—almost on bended knee—the one girl who can make his life complete. "My life is meaningless without you in it ... I want you as my wife." Hmmm ... will the real Marky please stand up?

From the sublime straight to the crass, bad-ass, ballsy, and brassy: "I Need Money" doesn't sugarcoat the message here. Cowriting credit (along with Donnie

"I Need Money" is the song that provokes this response!

and Marky) went to the renowned team of Gamble & Huff, as the song samples their tune "For the Love of Money." Marky raps, "Money is the thing I need to fulfill my greed...forget love and all that crap...I'm just trying to keep my pockets fat!" There's a reference to his own brother, "a millionaire who don't even share...I could be on welfare." When asked if he was really referring to Donnie, Marky said it was just a joke.

"The Last Song on Side B," was written, produced, and arranged by Donnie's closest New Kid buddy, Danny Wood. Along with a credited sample by the Jimmy Castor Bunch, Danny's contribution is a straight-up dance tune, a lively

ⓞⓞⓞⓞⓞⓞⓞ

Of the New Kids, "I suppose I get along with Danny Wood best, 'cause we work out at the same gym."

(Chris Mackie)

way to end the album. Except it doesn't exactly *end* it—the last line of the last song on side B reminds you that "It's just begun."

Music for the People was embraced by the record-buying people immediately. It hip-hopped onto Billboard's Top 200 record charts and hung tough for over 40 weeks, peaking at number 21. Not bad for a debut. But *Music for the People* meant much more to Marky than big numbers. In the end, he'd not only done exactly what he set out to do, but was rewarded with unexpected bounty. The record's greatest gift to its artist was this: just as a record is round, so this one took Donnie and Marky full circle. "It brought us back together," says Marky.

Good Vibrations— and Mixed Reviews

7

"Good Vibrations," the first single off *Music for the People*, was released in July 1991. It gave music critics their first chance for a shot at Marky: collectively, they took their best ones. To be fair, some critics *were*, and thoughtfully appraised the single and the album, giving both a generally positive reaction. Among the reviews Marky's mom probably has pasted in the family scrapbook was this one from the New York *Daily News*: "The music is *fun* . . . [We applaud him] for giving credit to Loleatta Holloway . . . It's enjoyable street music." *Billboard* chimed in with "Marky drops cost-conscious rhymes over a percolating hip-hop beat base" and "It's pure rap, with a pumped-up piano and flashy vocal hook. Marky's delivery should hit fast with the teeny rap set." Of the track "Wildside," a critic felt that "It goes a long way toward establishing a street-hip image for Marky." *Interview* magazine applauded it as ". . . a slugfest of contagious hip-hop and synthesized funk, from the spiritual calisthenics of 'Good Vibrations,' to the down and dirty "Bout Time I Funk You.' " *Entertainment Weekly*'s total review was mixed, but the positive part praised Marky for being "admirably willing to grapple with urban themes," and, the best of all: "Marky has the goods to lead rap music into its next artistic phase." Could've written that one himself!

Not so for the rest.

Even when they're expected, bad reviews hurt. Some attacked the music itself: " 'Good Vibrations,' is a pedantic rap single," wrote *Newsweek*, and *Rolling Stone*'s readers included "Good Vibrations" in its Worst Single of the Year category. Many more of the negative reviews went for Marky's throat. *Billboard* observed, "He's the latest entry into the hip-hop hunkasaurus market, pushing the beefcake." *Entertainment Weekly* chimed in with "He strains to keep the

(Chris Mackie)

"Your lyrical content needs to have meaning. Otherwise, keep it to yourself."

"In the beginning, I used to blame (the low-riding pants) on stupid stuff like not wearing a belt, or because (when I was a kid) I had to wear my brother's hand-me-downs. But that excuse doesn't work anymore."

(Marko Shark/LGI)

lyrics in tune with the beat... He's got a good heart, but sometimes, nice guys do finish last." And *Rolling Stone* readers put him in the Worst Male Singer slot (along with Michael Bolton, Axl Rose, Prince, and Vanilla Ice).

Marky's man enough to take the bad with the good—what drove him ballistic, however, were reviews that compared him to other pop stars. Vanilla Ice, and New Kids on the Block were, no surprise, the two most often cited. Unfortunately, *those* kinds of reviews were the most plentiful. "Marky enters Vanilla Ice territory with a lightweight pop/rap track," said one. "Marky is not a bad rapper and he *is* less obnoxiously egomaniacal than Vanilla Ice," opined another, but "He's a pale imitation of Vanilla Ice's simplistic pop-rap."

As might be expected, Marky had his *own* take on the reviewers, especially those who attacked *him*. "Listen to the music, man. We didn't put out *me*, we put out a record. Listen to the *music*, and then if you still don't like it, then, cool. But it's like, understand the music and understand what we're talkin' about, before you make an opinion of us, y'know what I mean?"

To "sample" a famous phrase, "But the little girls understood." They knew exactly what Marky meant. To prove it, they went out and bought the single . . . and bought the album . . . and bought each new succeeding single . . . and provided macho Marky with the kind of stats that fortify against critical sticks and stones. "Good Vibrations" soared to the top of Billboard's singles chart and became Marky's first number-one hit, selling over a million units. That was in the U.S.A. Then it shot up the charts in England, Germany, Sweden, Australia, Canada, Japan, Holland, and Denmark.

Marky's follow-up, "Wildside," which came out in November 1991, spent 20 weeks on the singles chart, and *10* weeks on the rap charts. It never went to number one in either place, but did go gold, selling in excess of 500,000 units. "I Need Money," released in February '92, didn't do quite as well, but made a respectable showing on the charts, debuting at number 83 and hanging in for eight weeks. "Peace" came out in April '92; it is Marky's personal favorite.

No question that the success of the singles was propelled by the videos. As one observer said, "The records began to imitate a rocket when MTV started touting them." Like many other hot-looking musicians, Marky benefitted immeasurably from the exposure afforded by not only MTV, but the Video Jukebox Network as well. But more than beefcake went into the videos. Marky had gotten his video feet wet by cameoing in New Kids' "Step by Step" and "Games" videos. When it came to do "Good Vibrations," he felt "completely comfortable" in front of the camera. It showed. Marky knew exactly how to strut his musical stuff to best advantage: so did the Funky Bunch. Loleatta Holloway—who became an honorary Funky Bunch member—appeared in the video as well.

"Good Vibrations," which was shot in three separate Boston locations and paid for by Marky and Donnie, became an MTV staple, one of the most heavily requested videos of the summer of '91. The follow-up shoots for "Wildside," and "I Need Money," which were filmed in Los Angeles, were no less impressive. All three were packaged, along with interviews and on-stage clips, in Marky's first long-form video, appropriately titled *Music for the People*, which came out in March 1992.

Marky expected the mixed reviews, and hoped for the success of the singles, videos, and ultimately, the album. What he never even dreamed about were the awards.

Onstage. "It's basically like a party-type situation."

(Chris Mackie)

(Marko Shark/LGI)

"I feel like a new person. I am doing things to better myself. Everything right now is like a dream come true."

But that's exactly what came next. The people showed their power and their approval, here in the U.S.A., and in Canada and England as well. In April 1991, before *Music for the People* even came out, Marky Mark and the Funky Bunch were voted Best New Rap Act at the Boston Music Awards. Mark's reaction: "Great! I didn't expect to win at all, we didn't even have a record out yet. But the fans knew us, and supported us. We're very excited. It's the most memorable experience of my career up until now."

More to come. In fact, Marky hip-hopped the hemisphere collecting accolades for his smash debut. Across the ocean in England, the readers of *Smash Hits* magazine voted for Marky Mark and the Funky Bunch as Best Dance Act,

Posin' with the world's oldest rock music writer, seventysomething Jane Scott of the *Cleveland Plain Dealer*— who loved the show!

(Janet Macoska)

1991. Flying over to accept the award, Marky burbled, "I can't believe it! I've won! This is the best award I could've won, the best category, too. I knew about the *Smash Hits* awards. I knew they was [*sic*] important because Donnie has always told me that *Smash Hits* is the 'mag daddy,' but I never really thought I'd get one this soon. Being a new group, you never know what people are gonna think, but now I'm really excited. I'm real glad we've taken off. This award is proof, man."

In April 1992, Marky once again took home a handful of Boston Music Awards—he won Best Single (for "Good Vibrations,") plus two for Best Pop CD and Best "R 'n' B" CD.

Canadian fans weighed in with their own proof by presenting Marky Mark and the Funky Bunch a platinum award for selling a million copies of *Music for the People* there. And back on American shores, in January 1992 Marky Mark and the Funky Bunch found themselves nominated in the Best New Rap Artist category at the people-powered American Music Awards (which are more a popularity contest than, say, the Grammys are). Although Marky's bunch lost out to Naughty by Nature, they were invited to come to the televised ceremonies and be presenters. Which they did, proof positive that, in spite of the negative, they really truly were on their way.

8

Meet the Funky Bunch

All professional rappers need backup support, dancers, deejays (scratchers), and vocalists—Marky never intended to be the exception. His personal sex appeal and talent notwithstanding, from the start his act was conceived of as a package deal, with as much emphasis on visuals (videos and the live show) as on the music and the message. To that end, Marky and his people looked for the baddest and the best, in Boston and beyond, to become the Funky Bunch.

The bunch was assembled, finally, by Mary Alford, with input from Marky, by referrals, recommendations, advertisements, and auditions. Some who made the cut were personal friends of Marky's; others he met for the first time at their auditions. All became part of the family.

The first hired was deejay/dancer Terry Yancey, whose "nom du rap" was DJ T, for obvious reasons. Terry was someone Mary had met several months before she began auditions for the Funky Bunch. Terry, in fact, had been dancing in front of a mirror (at a shoe store, no less), when Mary approached and got his number. She held on to it, and when the time was right, sent for him.

Terry, born on September 11, 1969, picked up the art of scratching from a friend and got his pre–Funky Bunch experience deejaying at home, on stage at school, and at neighborhood parties. He'd done time with a couple of "unofficial" groups, but the Funky Bunch is his first professional gig. A natural dancer and

When they first met, Terry Yancey thought Marky was going to be a stuck-up jerk...

(Chris Mackie)

... but he was soon disabused of that notion. Deejay and rapper got on famously from the get-go.

(Chris Mackie)

rapper, Terry helps out with the choreography and inter-raps with Marky in their show.

Marky's take on Terry: "He makes sure the sound holds up in the show, y'know, he keeps busy. He be dancin' and everything."

Once the deejay position was filled, three dancer slots were open.

Marky's ace dancer, Ashey Ace, was known at school as Anthony (Andy) Thomas. Ashey's birthday is November 21, he's single and in his mid–20s. Marky on Ashey: "Ashey is a mean knucklehead. He's on cloud nine. He sings in the show—tries to sing, anyway! He be doin' his part, y'know?"

Onstage with the Funky Bunch. "We dance, we sing, we rap, and we collaborate with Marky."

(Janet Macoska)

(Helen Bologna)

"People should expect a high-energy, action-packed, spur-of-the-moment show—every night something different. We've got a live band. It's a real exciting show. It has its very deep moments as well. But we're out to have a good time."

Scott Ross was the next dancer hired. Born on April 6, 1969, single dude Scott explains why his rap name is Scottie G.: "The 'G' stands for gifted, because I'm gifted with the power of stepping to the stage and bring all the mighty juices up there." Now that we've cleared that one up...

"My full name is Hector Barrows, Jr.," says the third dancer, "but I be called Hector-the-Bootie-Inspector because I inspects all the booties as they walk on by the Funky Bunch and Marky Mark." Hector was born on May 14, 1969, and is further credited by Marky: "Hector choreographs most of the dance stuff. He's a dancer who sings and raps in the show as well."

"It's not about black rap or white rap. If you can rap, you can rap. If you can't, you can't."

(Paul Lydon/LGI)

The Funky Bunch also features two female dancers, who go by the names of Marie and Ms. ?, *and* a pair of beefy bodyguards whose function is to stand on the side of the stage and look tough. Marky has tagged them "the Two Ministers of Security." Actually, they are Marky's buddies from the neighborhood, Rasta Phil and the Brizia. "They're cool, I've known them for years, they're my home-boys,'" says Mark.

Scottie G. sums up how the Bunch feel about Marky: "He's showing a true positive image that I would back up. I would go the distance with Mark."

In a much-published incident back in December of 1991, in fact, he and Ashey Ace almost had to. In Manchester, England, Scottie and Ashey came up against the ugly flip side of their dream jobs. As they were leaving a fast–food restaurant, they were jumped by four hoodlums. Ashey and Scottie were so savagely beaten that Marky Mark and the Funky Bunch had to cancel appearances opening for the New Kids in England.

What made the attack even worse was that it was clearly a case of bias: Ashey, whose leg was broken, and Scottie, who suffered a concussion and required stitches, are black. Their attackers were white. Reported a bystander, "They didn't stand a chance. The four thugs kicked them to the ground."

Thankfully, Scottie recovered fully and has put the incident well behind them. Ashey, however, did not fare as well. He had to leave the band temporarily to undergo knee and leg surgery. If he recovers fully he will rejoin the band.

9

Who's Dissin' Marky—and Why

To "dis'" in street slang, means to treat with disrespect, or criticize unfairly. For some reason, Marky Mark Wahlberg has come in for more than his fair share. Some of the knocks, of course, he expected, and responded to within the songs on *Music for the People*. There was no way, however, to prepare for the rest of what came his way. Here are some of the brickbats hurled at him, along with his best, or at least most earnest, defenses.

The argument that rap music is strictly an art form created by and belonging to African-Americans is not a new one. Marky's not only heard it, he's responded to it in several of his songs, most strongly in "So What Chu Sayin." Still, many in the black rap community aren't buying it—from Marky or anyone else. Their argument is that no white boy (or girl) has the right to rap, period. Not Vanilla Ice, not the Beastie Boys, not Third Bass, and surely not Mark Robert Wahlberg. Whites don't—they *can't*—know what it's all about. They just don't have the history, or the soul.

Marky doesn't dis, or miss, the point. "I feel for the ones who have worked so hard to pioneer this art form. And a lot of people haven't stayed true to it, don't have the respect and love for it that I do. There are a lot of white rappers out there who just don't belong in rapping," he acknowledges. He cites Vanilla

Ice as one of those, because "he didn't stay true to the art form," that by rapping about "cars, and a pound of bacon" (in "Ice, Ice, Baby"), Vanilla Ice not only commercialized and whitewashed rap, but in fact ridiculed it. And in that way, made it harder for any white rapper to be accepted and taken seriously by the black rap community. Marky distances himself, however, from Ice and other white rappers. "*My* music is very true to the art form. *I'm* not commercializing rap, or whitewashing it. I grew up in a predominately black neighborhood and went to predominately black schools. And hip-hop is what I grew up listening to. If you know what's up and are hip and on the money—like me—it doesn't matter who you are." He continues, "I'm proud to be white. I don't have anything against my color. But I don't think color matters, either. Just like I feel it doesn't matter that I'm a white dude doin' black music."

Mark's got a great ally in his brother Donnie, who discourses with ease on the black/white rap criticism leveled at his baby brother.

No doubt Donnie speaks for both Wahlbergs when he says, "You have to give respect to the music and where it came from. A lot of black artists started rock 'n' roll. Rock 'n' roll is now a white thing and when, say, (the black rock group) Living Colour came out, people found that strange. But black people really pioneered rock 'n' roll. Most of the popular music today came from gospel, and I think it's important to respect those roots. Someday it can easily be forgotten that rap music came from black people and it really did. Someday in the future you might read that the Beastie Boys started rap. That's gonna be a total disrespect to the roots of rap music. So it's important to always recognize where the music came from. I want that music to always be respected."

As Donnie detailed, the whole argument about whites ripping off black music goes much further back than Marky Mark and hip-hop. It's a variation on a very old theme—which doesn't make it any less true. White artists plagiarizing ideas from black musicians dates back to the days before Elvis Presley. Popular stars of the fifties were routinely accused of taking gospel, soul, and even jazz and diluting it with pop and country flavoring—and making millions popularizing it. In the 1960s, the Beatles admitted their main musical influence was, in fact, black American soul music. British artists like Eric Clapton and Jeff Beck have said that they identified with the anguish of great black musicians—and imitated them. And it is possible that many of today's white teens—like Marky—identify with the urban drama expressed in rap music.

So a precedent has been set. But is being a culture vulture acceptable? Was it ever? It's an argument that has merit and will rage on. Marky, at the moment, is the musician in the middle of it.

Unfortunately, Marky's had to answer for more than just the generic issue of

(Marko Shark/LGI)

"If I can make dope rap records, it doesn't matter what color I am."

race in rap music. Very specific fingers have been pointed at him, and those are the ones he's found toughest to refute. Marky's biggest problem has come, ironically, from the home front, from those he might've called his homeboys. For it's the fellas from his neighborhood, leveling the harshest charges. Those who might've been proudest that one of their own is making it are, in fact, angriest. They're calling Marky a thief.

A group called the RSO Crew, who've been rapping around neighboring Roxbury for eight years, have publicly accused Marky of pilfering their stage act. "Marky's whole act is a carbon copy of us," says a member of the Crew. "He's wearing [Boston] Bruins outfits like us, black and gold colors, just like us. He even copied our stage moves and our idea to use bodyguards in cowhide jackets onstage as part of the act."

RSO's allegations have been echoed by yet another Beantown rap group, calling themselves Posse NFX, who say, "We believe he's taken a lot of musical grooves and show maneuvers from us. Marky's found a way to make money at our expense!"

Although Marky has not answered these specific charges in public, he *has* stood by his stock statement: "I'm not taking anything away from other rappers. I just feel I can make dope records..."

This is another charge that's cropped up repeatedly, most vociferously, once again, from the folks back in Boston. The publisher of a respected hip-hop magazine, the *Source*, who is also a concert promoter and former deejay, frankly doubts Marky's claims of authenticity. "I don't know Mark's whole history," he says, "but I do know from being around the Boston hip-hop scene since 1986 that he was never in any way involved."

Marky's claim that he is a tough guy from the streets—on record, in videos, and in the flesh—is being dissed as well. One of the RSO Crew bodyguards was quoted in a Boston newspaper, "[When I saw Marky] I was disgusted. *We've* been out there on the streets. *We've* lost friends, brothers. *We* know how it feels to go to ten funerals in a year. Then along comes Marky, claiming he's like us."

Another RSO member also went on record in the papers saying, "In Marky's videos, he tries to present this image of coming from the streets, walking around with bodyguards, hooded sweatshirts, and Bruins gear—those are things that RSO Crew did, back when hip-hop first came to Boston."

"He's just another kid with a family with money," says another longtime observer of the Boston rap scene. "All that stuff about hanging out in the streets is just another Vanilla Ice story [i.e., falsehood]."

An old friend of Marky's comes to his defense on this one. John Mahoney, who is himself a musician and knew Marky back at Copley High School, says

"I don't want to get too big..."

"no fair." "It's all jealousy stuff," he figures. "[It's true that] Mark wasn't a *real* punk and never got into fights in high school, but he *was* raised in Dorchester. He *has* been in the ghetto. He knows what he's talking about."

Marky himself takes the offense. "[Rough raps] could be made by anybody who is going through [rough times]. I question a lot of rappers, whether they are really as hard as they say. A lot of people don't even question if NWA [one of the most raw and controversial rap groups around] is for real. Just because they're from Compton [in Los Angeles], does that prove they were really in gangs and stuff? They question me 'cause I'm white, but they don't think to doubt others,

Crotch-grabbing on stage: a trademark.

(John Paschal/Celebrity Photo)

(Janet Gough/Celebrity Photo)

"I try to show 'em the joint, so maybe I can get a little bit of juice back at the hotel..." (a quote from his long-form video, Music for the People).

just because they're black. Frankly, I think a lot of those brags in raps are a bunch of bull."

What may really rankle others is Marky's success. He's perceived as making millions, while those from whom he allegedly stole are still on street corners. "We can't get a gig," say the Posse NFX. That *is* a sore point in the rap community, that many hardworking, talented artists can't get a break, while someone like Marky seems to have walked right into fame and fortune, without (in their view) trying very hard at all.

Some think it just goes back to the whole issue of race all over again. "It's easier for white rappers," says a black rapper, "just like it was with jazz and rock 'n' roll. Whites came along and took jazz and rock 'n' roll from blacks. It hurts when this happens, because we've worked hard for many years, then someone comes along and takes the glory for it."

Another country heard from: the older generation, some of whom happen to be the parents of the kids who've embraced Marky, his attitude, *and* his underwear. A newspaper columnist, clearly a member of the former and not much of a rap fan, had this reaction after watching Marky in performance: "The kid's arrogance was definitely hard to take. There he was, this shirtless, crotch-grabbing, young man, screaming indecipherable words to some ridiculous rap song, while the dancers and [Loleatta Holloway], were relegated to the stage behind him. His forte is his ability to talk and grab his crotch at the same time. And that is all he does.

"The message," she concluded, "is not just that sex is a 'Let's do it cuz it feels good thing,' but that cockiness, arrogance, and power are the real aphrodisiacs, and ability and talent don't count at all."

Of course, it's the very fact that their parents do *not* understand or approve of Marky that makes him all the more attractive to his young fans. He then becomes, like Mick Jagger and Jim Morrison before him, forbidden fruit—or, in his case, forbidden Fruit of the Loom.

10

Takin' It to the Streets

Marky's record had proved itself; so had the videos. Now it was up to the rapper himself—could he prove it all night long on the concert stage? Could Marky draw the crowds, get his *people* to pack the halls? Could he work them into a frenzy with his music, his raps, his dancing, his sex appeal? Yo, who you kidding? There are no sure bets in show biz, but Marky, even just starting out, was about as close as it gets.

After all, there was a ready-to-rock contingent who already knew him, and were primed to pack his shows. Those would be the girls who saw Marky as, perhaps, New Kids: The Next Generation. By the time Marky was ready to hit the road, even they realized his music wasn't what they'd been raised on, but responded to his lineage, his looks, and the musical hooks all the same. Much as Mark appreciated that support, he was hoping to attract a more hard-core following as well. To that end, he'd fashioned a show that, like the music, had more rough edges than smooth curves, was more blatantly sexual than teasingly provocative.

Working with Mary Alford as coordinator, Donnie as overseer, and the Funky Bunch choreographing, Marky sweated his buns off to get the moves and the music happening for the concert stage.

The first test runs were out of town—make that way out of town—and were almost guaranteed to go down well. For Marky Mark and the Funky Bunch did open for New Kids at the end of '91 in England, when it was still swollen with New Kids fever. To the British boppers, any friend of NKOTB was a friend of theirs. Marky Mark and the Funky Bunch's stage debut was a resounding success. Unfortunately, it was also abbreviated. Marky got sick overseas, the Funky Bunch got attacked, and they all had to return home to recuperate after only a couple of gigs.

It was disappointing, but not a crusher. After all, the big test was really at home, on his first real tour, that would take him through the U.S.A., from January to June 1992. His tour bookers worked fast and furiously to that end. As Marky saw it just before he hit the road, "We got so much stuff booked, I don't even know where it is!"

Where it *was* included clubs and mid-size venues up and down the east coast. There was a three-day stop in Florida that included a Disney World gig and the MTV Spring Break party in Daytona Beach. On that road trip, Marky not only did concerts, but made promotional pit stops at radio stations and record stores. There were photo sessions—including the one for the famous *Interview* magazine cover—and meetings with the press in every town. There were, of course, the fans, clamoring for a glimpse of the newest, and by far sexiest, rap hero. For a novice, Marky took it all in stride, handling the pressures, the praise, and the long hours with amazing aplomb.

Like most rockers or rappers on the road, Marky travels from gig to gig in a caravan of trucks (for his stage equipment) and tour buses. His own bus, as befits the star, is luxurious. It includes a kitchen area up front, with fridge, microwave, table, bench seats, TV, and VCR. Six bunk beds (three high) take up the middle of the bus, while Marky's private quarters are in the back. That's the place for his personal boom box (rap music is always blasting from it), phone, TV, VCR, and sitting area. If he wants solitude, that's where he goes on those long all-night rides between gigs.

Marky's never alone on the bus. Aside from his driver, at least one of his bodyguards is always with him. There's room, of course, when members of his family decide to hop aboard for a leg of the trip, or for personal friends as well. In fact, those bus rides tend to be a good time for Marky to catch up with the people in his life that he's close to.

Marky generally arrives at the venue of the evening a good four or five hours before show time. Sound checks, stage setups, and rehearsals are all part of the daily grind. And this, too: Marky's become quite a perfectionist over the past six months. He's gone, in fact, from the almost passive student-novice to a take-

The view from the limo—thumbs up to the fans outside.

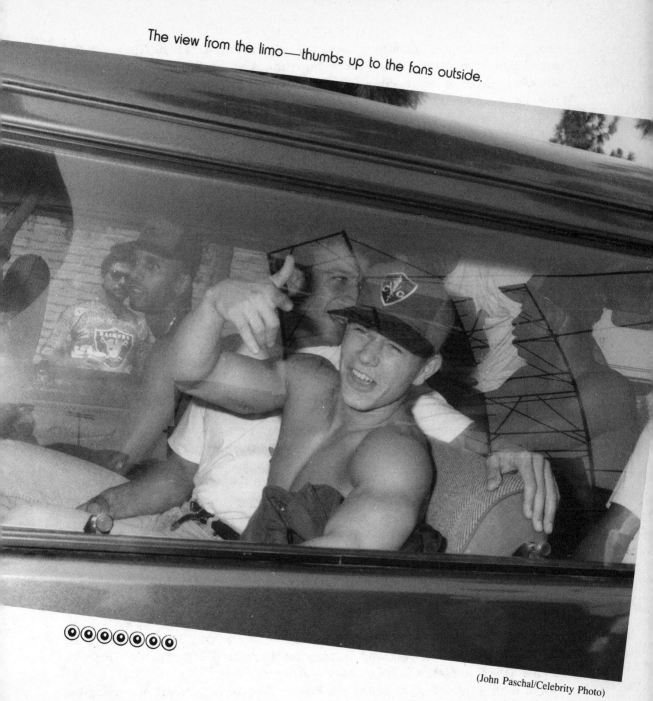

charge tour leader, admonishing everyone to "get it right." He huddles with the sound guys, the lighting crew, his video team. And macho Marky, the star of the whole shebang, has even been spied from time to time tidying up the stage, moving instruments and equipment exactly into place, even tossing away a used coffee cup or scrap of paper.

Knowing Marky, it's no surprise that he walks around backstage in his underwear, but another side of his personality, rarely seen in public, *is* on display during those quiet moments. That's the mellow Marky, sitting by himself on the edge of the stage, bare feet dangling, dreamily strumming a guitar. There's no sign of the raging rapper at those times. And to an observer, Marky seems, in many ways, most at home, confident and even peaceful when he's looking out on a completely empty auditorium.

He may be in his own world at times, but he's never really by himself for long. As show time draws nearer, more and more people saunter in. Aside from the band, his bodyguards, Funky Bunch, and technical crew, backstage passes go to his tour manager, Miguel Melendez, assorted roadies, plus support staff like his wardrobe and hair and makeup people, and the caterers.

Of the last, Marky is quite specific about his needs. Unlike the legendary prima donna rock stars before him, Marky's demands on the road are few. In fact, Marky has only *one* major requirement for his well-being: food. Aside from the "transgression" of the sugary Lucky Charms cereal for breakfast—every morning—it's a healthy menu for Mark, day in and day out. With little variation, his pre-concert dinner is plain, dry turkey (hold the mayo) or plain, boneless chicken or canned tuna, with a baked potato and fresh fruit. Although he doesn't impose his strict regime on the crew, there is one set-by-Marky rule: no soda backstage for any of the performers. A $50 fine is levied for anyone caught with a contraband can. Marky downs instead mineral water, juices, or a fruity health-food concoction that includes protein powder, fresh pineapple, and crushed ice. It's not so much for weight control that Marky watches what he eats ["My metabolism just burns everything off," he says], but to keep that brawny body buff.

After the arrival of the Funky Bunch and Marky's posse, the backstage mood changes completely. Gone is the mellow Mark, replaced by the fun-loving, frequently over-the-top rapper his fans have come to know and embrace.

For the most part, it's a boys' club backstage at a Marky Mark show. It's not that there are no women allowed, just that few happen to be part of this particular scene. Many, in fact, would probably feel out of place.

For there's more than the requisite boys-will-be-boys jamming and jiving between Marky and the Bunch. Ashey, Scottie, Hector, Terry, and Mark play rough games of floor hockey in the hallways (they bring their own equipment) and bounce impromptu down-and-dirty raps (sometimes accompanied by lewd gestures) off each other—and oftentimes, off the walls too—in a macho game of one-upsmanship to see who can be the most outrageous. Between the five of them, it's often a toss-up.

There's more irreverence where that came from. The boys shamelessly mimic other performers—their version of Hammer's "Pray," for example, displays major attitude.

(Helen Bologna)

Tour manager Miguel Melendez used to work for the New Kids. Now he's exclusive to the Mark tip!

Every once in a while, of course, they cool it. That's when special guests— like Marky's mom Alma, or even his parish priest, Father Flavin—visit backstage. (Both often do.) Although Marky could never be accused of going "respectable," he and the Bunch do know when to tone it down.

In the final hour or so before he goes on, Marty plays host to journalists and photographers backstage, as well as the occasional superstar musician who happens to be playing in the same town. Van Halen visited when Marky was in South Carolina one night, and Marky returned the compliment by catching their show the next.

"I never thought (fame) was this bad. I find myself cuddled up on a little chair in an airport, or sleeping under a table, trying to get a little rest (while) everyone thinks I'm this millionaire..."

(Paul Lydon/LGI)

"People think I'm on some island, with a mansion, but I'm really in Little Rock, Arkansas, doing three shows a night, and traveling by bus."

Do fans ever get backstage passes? Not a show goes by without a slew of the lucky ones getting to stick that coveted VIP patch onto their jeans. Most often, Marky will meet and greet winners of radio station, TV, or record company promotional contests, or fans who are lucky enough to know someone who knows someone with connections. At a prescribed pre-show time, Marky meets backstage with the fans, signs autographs, poses for Polaroids, and bestows hugs and kisses in healthy doses. For his fans, those few moments with Marky provide memories for a lifetime: for Marky, it's when he meets with other kinds of concertgoers—the kids who are handicapped, or seriously ill, or homeless—that fills his heart with joy. Knowing the good he can do for others is a big part of what it's all about. Marky's reminded of it at every show.

Just seconds before show time, at every gig, Marky leads his performers in a quiet, heartfelt prayer session. Everyone gathers round in a circle as Marky asks for the Lord's blessing on the about-to-begin concert.

Is he ever nervous just before hitting the stage? Not that he'll admit to. "What's there to be nervous about?" he asks. "I'm excited, I like to get really crazy ill—I feel more like I'm just gonna blow before I go out there!"

And so it is, with a heart bursting with love and excitement, the music blasting and raps going around full-tilt in his head, that Marky Mark and the Funky Bunch hit the stage running.

Make that: running, jumping, karate-kicking, and cartwheeling into the spotlight. Marky is backed by a live band that includes a drummer, percussionist, bass player, guitarist, and two keyboard players. As the Funky Bunch, covered from top to toe in shiny sweatsuits, do slickly choreographed somersaults, Marky, with mike to mouth, swaggers, mugs, and struts his stuff. He may come out fully dressed, but before too long, he's frequently shirtless—and *always* shameless. As the band percolates, the deejay scratches, and the Funky Bunch pumps up the jam, Marky grabs his crotch and bursts into his opening number—appropriately, "Marky Mark Is Here." There's no doubt about it, Marky Mark is definitely in the house tonight!

"Get ready for the most unbelievable, most action-packed show ever!" Marky often exhorts his audience. "It'll be the best thing you've ever seen!" It's no idle boast.

For the next 75 minutes, between the push-ups and the preening, the bumping, grinding, butt-wiggling, and crotch-grabbing, Marky performs most of the songs on his album, from the crowd-pleasing "Good Vibrations" (if Loleatta Holloway's not there, Stacy X, from Ex-Girlfriend, does the vocal honors) to the chilling "Wildside," the romantic "Make Me Say Ooh!" and the sexy "'Bout Time I Funk You." During "On the House Tip," Marky invites the crowd to "Move your body! Dance!"—and they do. When he does "I Need Money," those who can get close enough attempt to stuff bills in his briefs and hurl coins at him. Marky comes close to the edge of the stage and extends his arms, to touch as many of the faithful as possible. Throughout the show, the adoring throw flowers, stuffed animals, and—a sign of the times and of Marky's message—condoms as well. (At one concert, Marky started the audience in a chant: "Safe sex! Safe sex!") They bring signs and banners, many unprintable here, others bearing messages like "Marky Gives Good Vibrations" and "Marky Mark Makes Me Go 'Ooh'!"

Marky's audience is usually a balance of girls and boys, pin–striped men and women, blacks and whites. It's a show that brings people together. They may come from all strata, but they all come for the same reason. They come for the music and the message, the raps and the rush, to dance in their seats, scream their lungs out, and, sometimes, even faint from the overwhelming excitement. Most especially, of course, they come for the spectacle.

Marky doesn't disappoint on any count. He knows, full well, exactly what the crowd really wants. And what they want, he's more than ready to give: from a tease of torso with just a few inches of the elastic waistband on his Calvin Kleins showing, to an all-out, up-front-assault, complete drop of his drawers.

Marky's crowd has come to expect it; they want flesh, and Marky's made the show of *his* very much a part of his *show*. Marky confesses, "I do it every night. Every night I pull my pants down. It's unbelievable, people go crazy. Sometimes they rush the stage." On one memorable occasion, he came out and started the show in a bathrobe—only to rip it off and expose his famous briefs. Marky clearly gets off on the crowd reaction—the louder they cheer, the lower his pants go. "What I like about Mark," mused a teensomething fan, "is that, you know, when he pulls his pants down, you can almost see . . . everything!" And in fact, Marky's show does come teasingly close to an X rating: like his album and his video, perhaps it should be advertised with a parental advisory. Only in addition to "Explicit lyrics," it might say "Close-to-explicit body parts." (In fact, in a first-ever move, his Pay-Per-View concert was tagged with a parental-discretion advisory.)

Nothing the audience does, or *he* does, embarrasses Marky. The music, the moves, the reaction—all feel natural and seem spontaneous. (According to those who've seen the show at various venues, however, it's exactly the same each time, down to the last kick and cartwheel.) He doesn't forget the words to his raps, or the dance routines. His worst moment came when he totally blanked out on what city he was in, and yelled out, with great enthusiasm, "Hello, Pittsburgh!"—in Cleveland.

A rare McDonald's break on the bus.

Marky's post-show routine varies little. After taking his bows, he towels off the bodacious sweat he's worked up, jumps into a waiting limo, and zips off to a pre-booked, nearby hotel for the night. In cities where fans have found out where he's staying, he's often a virtual prisoner there. That happened for the first time in England, where Marky lamented, "The girls wouldn't let me do nothin'! They were so crazy, followin' me around everywhere, I had to stay in the hotel!" By now, however, he's gotten used to that kind of scene and has even figured out a few strategies to ensure his privacy.

Marky's posse generally books an entire floor at the hotel. When necessary,

"Drug-free is the way to be." Marky makes healthy eating and drinking part of his daily regimen.

(Paul Lydon/LGI)

bodyguards are posted at each elevator door—making sure that no one gets out on Marky's floor without a room key to prove they belong there. In Daytona Beach, during MTV's Spring Break performance, Marky proved so popular, *10* security guards were needed to man the hotel.

There's no way Marky could just go to sleep after a performance. His internal engine is too revved up. Instead, after a quick shower, Marky often finds out where the hottest dance club in town is and parties till the wee hours.

The day after a concert, Marky will always work out at the gym before boarding the bus to his next gig. He tries to stay at hotels that are health-club-equipped, but when that's not possible, he heads for the nearest gym. Marky has mastered the machines that pump up his pecs and flatten his stomach. Those bulging biceps come from rigorous daily workouts.

Beyond a gym stop, there's little that Marky usually has time for when he's on the road. On rare occasions, if he's playing in a city for several days, he and the Bunch may relax by the hotel pool, hang out in the video-game room, or head for the nearest mall. That's the extent of their interest in or time for sightseeing. As he re*Mark*ed—as only he can—to the British press, who tried to show him world-famous sights like the Tower of London and the Palladium, "I'm not hip to your English culture . . . I don't know nothin'!"

For the most part, there's precious little time in Marky's packed schedule to *get* hip to the culture scene. Before he knows it, he's off to the next gig.

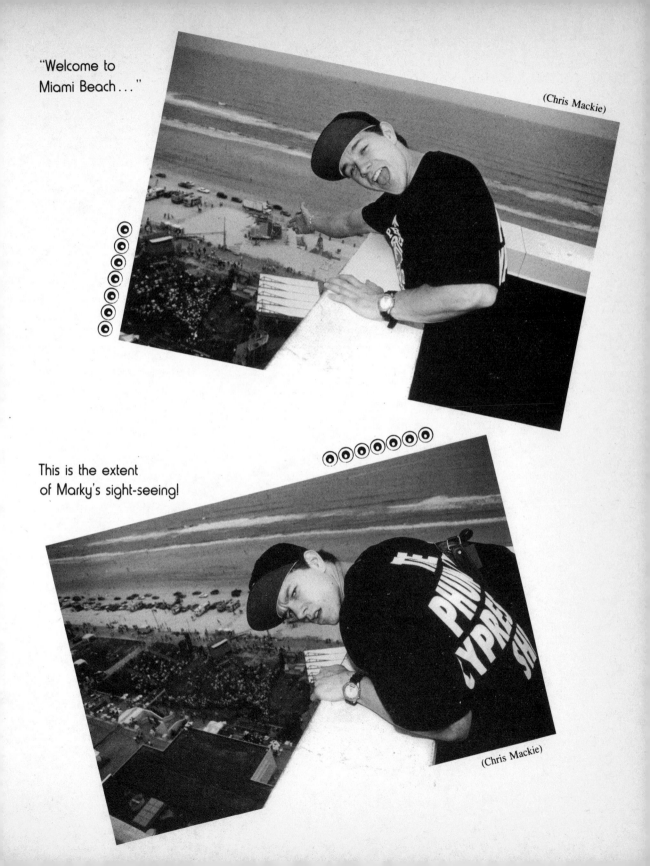

"Welcome to Miami Beach…"

(Chris Mackie)

This is the extent of Marky's sight-seeing!

(Chris Mackie)

11

Style and Substance

It isn't easy for a performer to carve out an identity that's uniquely his own. Marky's done it in a seemingly spontaneous combustion of mind, music, body, soul, attitude, and style. So far, no one's confused Marky Mark with anyone else.

He wears the same clothes—or lack of them—pretty much all the time, on stage as well as off. When he *is* dressed, it's nearly always in jeans or denim overalls (no shirt underneath) and what he terms "keen jackets." They may run the gamut from leather to rhinestone-studded to baseball silk, most often bearing the insignia of the Boston Celtics, Marky's hometown team of choice.

No shoes or biker boots for Mark; sneakers are the only footwear he feels comfortable in. "I got about 100 pairs," he told the press. "You gotta have fly sneakers. I usually wear Adidas. All my sneakers are stacked on the wall, on shelves." Considering that Marky was a kid who grew up wearing Donnie's worn-out sneakers, he certainly has compensated.

A Marky style staple is some kind of hat. He used to only wear baseball caps and has over 200 in his collection. "My favorite is the Minnesota Twins hat. It's just got an M in the front, so it's kind of like my logo," Mark mentioned a few months back. Lately, however, he's taken to covering his recently buzzed head

How low can he go? Just watch!

with hooded jackets and ski caps. Even those have logos. For the filming of his long-form video, Marky modeled a black White Sox (baseball) cap. Since Marky started wearing them, they've become very cool.

As Marky covers his noggin, so the Funky Bunch follows suit. Off stage, the guys usually wear brimmed hats or baseball caps; on stage, it's colorful bandanas all around.

And then there's his underwear.

Whether he's chosen boxers or briefs, showing them off to his fans has become a statement of style that's all his. Perhaps Marky didn't quite invent it—he credits Guns N' Roses' Axl Rose with doing the same thing—but Marky sure wins in the popularity polls for it, pants down.

Of course, when dissecting Mark's mode, the obvious feature is more substance than style. He has worked to create an almost perfectly sculpted chest, with bulging biceps and, as one reviewer put it, "a stomach as rippled as a potato chip." His close-to-exhibitionistic display of his buff upper body is a large part of what sets him apart from other young rappers and performers. For, as any fan knows, Marky performs, poses, and preens shirtless at every possible opportunity.

"The only reason I show my body off is because I work hard," claims Marky. That it's become part of his persona is just a perk. If it helps his popularity, and he likes to do it, why ask why?

In fact, Marky started working out not so much as a ploy to attract fans, but simply to lose weight. "When I quit smoking, I started eating like a pig," the ever-forthright Mark explains. "I put on 30 pounds in two months. So I joined a gym, right down the street from my house, and started to work out. It was really painful at first, but once I got over the initial difficulty of changing my life-style—I changed my eating habits, too—I found I could really put my whole self into working out at the gym."

Marky's become such a convert that he is at his most effusive when discussing his regime and what it does for him. In addition to bench-pressing and working the Stair Master, says Marky, "I lift weights every day for an hour and a half. I do free weights and lots of dumbbells for shaping and size. The heaviest weight I've lifted is about 300 pounds. Every other day, I work on my chest and triceps. Other days, I'll do my back and biceps, then my legs and shoulders. My legs are the weakest part, but I'm working on them!"

He's proud of the results, physically *and* mentally. "My arms are about 16 and a quarter inches. I have a 31-inch waist, and 16-and-a-quarter-inch-biceps.

"I work out to look good, but I also
do it to feel good about myself."

Yo, if you've got it
—flaunt it!

(Marko Shark/LGI)

I'm not too sure about my chest, but it's beginning to look good. I don't wanna be so big that I can't move around, I just wanna stay fit.

"It's very important to me to stay fit, it's good for stage presence, just to feel good.

"Along with working out, I try to eat a lot of protein, like chicken. And I avoid fatty food. When I gave up smoking, I used to stuff the food in my mouth to replace the cigarettes. Now, I eat real well. I'll never go back to cigarettes and food binges.

(Chris Mackie)

"It takes self-discipline, but you need that. And it gives you more drive and inspiration. I couldn't give it up now, I wouldn't want to. I feel so good!"

In a motivational mood, Marky concludes, "You've gotta be dedicated and work hard. Concentration and dedication are the important things."

12

Comin' Home

When he's off the road, Marky comes home—to Mom. In spite of his age, just 21, and newly minted superstar status, Marky continues to live with his family. Aside from mom Alma and stepdad Mark Conroy, that includes Donnie, too, when he's not on tour. Of course, these days, home is a far cry from the cramped Dorchester apartment Marky grew up in. About two years ago, Donnie used some of his New Kids fortune to purchase a spacious, modern home in Braintree, a pricey suburb of Boston. There's a swimming pool and Jacuzzi in the backyard, and, for the boys, a regulation-height basketball hoop. A six-foot-high fence has been erected around the entire house.

Much as Marky dislikes the fence, he understands full well the need for it: ever since a local newspaper printed his address, hordes of fans have stopped by—and, just like it used to be in the old house, often in the middle of the night. At least now the "visitors" can't get to the front door. "It's nice to be able to sleep at night without having constant knocking on the front door and windows," Marky said.

There's little motivation to move out on his own because he's got everything he needs right there, including plenty of privacy. Only occasionally does his mom revert to treating him like a kid. Alma does get embarrassed about Marky's pants-down stage act, but rather than be outwardly critical, "She leaves belts all

(Robin Kennedy/London Features)

A touch football game relieves tension
on the road. Marky's a natural athlete.

On the basketball court, Marky shows 'em what he's made of: muscle and hustle.

(Janet Gough/Celebrity Photo)

over my room, as a reminder." Marky has said. While the point is made, Marky has no intention of dropping his act.

His room "is like a little apartment. Kinda small, really. But it's got a fireplace and kitchen and it's full of sneakers and hats. I have a video game in there, Pac-Man. Upstairs is my mother's half of the house and that's where we have a huge TV screen that comes down from the ceiling—it's eight feet by eight feet. It's the best for watching boxing."

The new house in Braintree has become the central gathering spot for all the Wahlbergs, especially around the holidays. And Marky is still very close with all his brothers and sisters and their families. When he's on the road, he calls them all the time, but there's nothing to compare with the hugs and kisses he gets when he's home.

Back on his home turf, Marky delights in climbing behind the wheel of his black-on-black Jeep Cherokee, the one Donnie bought him a year ago, and blazing down the streets of Boston. It's much more than transportation—"It's my favorite place to be in the whole world," Marky confides. The best thing about it, in fact, is the stereo system he installed. "It's the most unbelievable sound system you ever heard," he boasts. "I put $10,000 into my car's system. I have 18 10-inch sub-woofers, five amplifiers, 1,000 watts of power. Shit-hot. The money came from my record budget, money I got from doin' shows, y'know. I got the pumpin' beats in my Jeep. Most of the records that are wack get thrown out the window." Those that don't include perennial favorites Bell Biv DeVoe plus less mainstream groups like Eric B. & Rakim, Sun King, and Brand Nubian.

Riding shotgun are most likely to be the people Marky dubs "my homeboys." Some are, indeed, old friends from the neighborhood, but in fact, Marky's posse is mostly made up of the guys involved with him musically. In Mark's world, the line between personal friends and business buddies is very much blurred; there's constant crossover. Old friends now work as security for Marky Mark and the Funky Bunch; Chuck D., from his management team, is now a personal friend.

When he's not playing music, Marky's playing sports. When the urge strikes and friends stop by the house, Marky gets up a friendly game of touch football, foozball, pool, or floor hockey. By himself, he often shoots hoops in the backyard, or goes one-on-one with Donnie.

(Janet Gough/Celebrity Photo)

13

On the Hype Tip

Even when he's home, it's hard for Marky to truly get away from it all. For he is firmly entrenched on what the New Kids used to call "the hype tip"—the express train to fame, fortune, and frenzied fans. Especially when he's back in Boston, where he's considered very much the local hero, Marky can't really get off.

Marky can't say, as Donnie might have, that he wasn't prepared for the spotlight, and the avalanche of attention and hype that came with it. Being a relative, and a cute, talented one, of the New Kids made Marky a favorite teen magazine subject. Mark Wahlberg—not Marky Mark, hunky leader of the Funky Bunch—was profiled in print and in pictures; before the boxers and bulging biceps, without benefit of a recording contract, he was already a familiar and even adored face.

From the start, however, Mark has maintained that being famous was not what buttered his muffin. "I don't need to be as big as the New Kids," offered Mark back in 1991. When fame came his way, he treated it gingerly . . . and warily. "The fame and the hype, it's not my thing," he repeated countless times over, in response to endless press queries. "I am dealing with it, it's OK, but it's not what I strive for, or what I always wanted. If hype is all I wanted, I would have stayed with the New Kids. Really, all I wanted to do is just make rap records, and that is all I'm doing. And now they are hits, so these other things are coming along with it—and these girls, and the sex symbol thing.

"But the fame thing is weak, and the sex symbol thing is weak. It all comes along with the success of my record, I know that, but it's really all a pain in the ass."

He's in a position to know—more than most, perhaps—that fame is often fleeting; it's the work that counts. "Success can come and go like the New England weather," Mark philosophizes. "You never know what's going to happen.

Signing a banner for Jammin' 92 radio. Marky took his time and really did an elaborate job. "I haven't done graffiti in years," he said. "This is fun."

(Janet Macoska)

(Marko Shark/LGI)

"I can be a real jerk when I'm tired. I need lots of sleep."

So I don't spend a lot of time thinking about it, I think about my record instead, and then the next one after that."

The direct by-product of fame that Marky can't help but think about, of course, is its human manifestation: the fans. In that arena, too, he had plenty of experience. "I'm used to the fans going crazy for Donnie, at every gas station and corner store he goes into. And I've had my share of fans screaming and yelling and waking me up in the middle of the night."

At first, he was concerned that his chief appeal lay in being Donnie's brother. But when he realized that the fan mania was for him, he was duly appreciative.

Affecting an attitude for the cameras. But Marky maintains, "I have a shy side, too."

(Marko Shark)

But appreciation has not gone over the edge to conceit. Mark maintains, "Fans don't boost my ego, I'm just glad they like my music."

Mark's fans come in all colors, shapes, sexual orientations, and sizes; he acknowledges and welcomes all of them, regardless, and aims to please them all. A special tenderness takes over, however, when he meets the youngest and least able of the lot backstage. He pays extra attention to the little kids, and has often been heard making up personal raps for them.

Those fans who aren't lucky enough to get a backstage pass still have a shot at meeting Mark. Some have learned to locate him on the road, and wangle reservations at the hotels he stays at. Others "bump into" him by showing up hours early at the concert venue and hanging out at the stage door; they know he's got to show up for an afternoon sound check.

Marky does many promotional appearances, often sponsored by local radio stations, a prime place for fans to get that coveted kiss, autograph, and snapshot. Marky minds none of this. "I got the girls nice and calm and relaxed," he told a journalist. "I hang out with them because they're out there all the time. They just want to get glimpses."

Before he dove into the fray himself, Marky used to pick up pocket change by working at the New Kids Fan Club headquarters. There, he'd read and help respond to the avalanche of letters that poured in daily. Now, more than half are addressed to him. Although he no longer hangs out at the fan club offices, Marky's well aware of the love and support sealed in those missives—he doesn't dismiss a single one. As much as possible, Marky reads his mail. He dictates personal answers when time allows, and occasionally, if a fan has included a phone number, he has even called.

(Helen Bologna)

◉◉◉◉◉◉◉

During MTV's Spring Break concert, Marky met the press. He traded quips with Youthquake's Jennifer and gamely did the promo thing.

14

Who Makes Marky Go "Ooh!"?

The attraction between Marky and the opposite sex is powerful, physical, very real—and very calculated. The appeal might be there even without the raw sexual energy of his concerts, but his outrageously suggestive gestures onstage leave little doubt as to his intent (and to little else). The shirtless strutting, pelvic thrusting, bumping, grinding, crotch-grabbing, and pants-dropping may well be precisely choreographed—but it has the desired effect. Every time out.

For what's become obvious over the past year is that Marky's talent extends way beyond his music. His ability to drive his audience into a steamy, sweaty, screaming frenzy—or, as *he* might put it (in fact, as he *did*, on his album), "make them say ooh!"—is reaching legendary proportions. Marky, in fact, by design or happenstance, has marketed himself as a hunk, a studly package few can resist. His effect isn't limited to prepubescent princesses. It knows no age boundaries. There are innocent babes who dream of chaste kisses, cuddles, and an autograph. There are the bolder batch who leave him love notes, with their phone numbers, attached to very personal items. There are women who come right out and (on hand-painted banners) say exactly what it is that Marky does for them (and what they'd like to do for him). Even Madonna, the brashest babe of all, reportedly wants his body (or so it's been printed).

Some fans take action. They hang around outside his hotel, or by the backstage entrance to the concert hall, hoping for an introduction. Others dream up sneaky schemes to come into direct contact; one girl hid inside a hotel laundry basket and jumped out when he walked down the hallway. Another, in Boston, followed him in her car. There are few places Marky can go without being surrounded and reminded of his very real appeal.

Not that he minds. All that much, anyway. For when it comes to Marky and the girls, the attraction is mutual. He *is* an outrageous flirt, on or off stage, and very much appreciates and is flattered by the attention. "The girls now, it's cool, it's a good feeling. I can handle it," he says, winking.

He insists, however, that it doesn't go to his head, that above the belt, he understands what's going on here. "I think the girls are just reacting to the show, maybe to the music a little bit. But I think it was just a reaction to the performance." Does he really believe that without his onstage actions, he'd be less of a sex symbol? In a rare moment of either candor or modesty, Marky told a reporter, "I'm no hunk. I'd give myself a two out of ten for my looks."

Marky's uncharacteristic lapse of bravado may be rooted in his teen experiences. Back then, he got burned, at least once. He admitted, "I have been in love, once or twice. Well, once. A few years ago, when I was between 16 and 18. It felt shitty, after the way it turned out. It's hard to describe." His hurt was probably made worse by comparisons to his big brother Donnie who, according to Mark, "always got the girls." Marky had his posse and his following, but while he was sometimes a dud, Donnie was ever the stud.

That, however, was then. Marky's clearly making up for lost time, big time. Although he is very much single and unattached, Marky is not without female companionship, especially when he's on the road. In fact, many of those who try *do* get to meet and spend time with the object of their desire. But despite his ready-for-anything stage demeanor, off stage he's a bit more circumspect. In a private moment with a fan who was holding a very explicit banner (saying what she'd like to do with him), Marky gently told her, "You really don't want to be holding up a sign like that."

He's careful about getting too involved with people he knows he may see only once. During an interview, he was asked about the best advice his mother ever gave him. He answered, only half-flippantly, "Wear two condoms!" Indeed, Marky has been quite candid about the importance of practicing safe sex. He preaches that message to his fans as well.

His experiences on the road have been mostly positive, even sweet on occasion. But no one he's met so far has managed to capture his heart. Nor does he

"You know, I get all choked up from time to time.
Like if I meet a beautiful girl, I might get shy."

expect it. In fact, Marky is especially wary of falling for a fan. "It would leave me wondering why she was interested in me. You never know what girls want from you, do you? I'm always on the lookout for a nice girl, but I can't see myself finding anyone until I come off the road."

Despite the ease of meeting women, Marky insists that being a rap star makes it harder, not easier, to find someone he could really be interested in. Certainly, spending so much time on his music and his career leaves little time to devote to a relationship. As one of his Funky Bunch put it, "You're just gone a lot, and girls get jealous of others you meet on the road . . . and they get fed up waiting for you."

Marky feelings are really mixed: "It's on my mind a lot, but . . . sometimes I feel I can't be with no girl. She might bring me down from all this. She might mess me up. She didn't really help me get here." Still, he seems to be looking: "I need a girlfriend bad. I'm in search for a girl, the right girl."

Marky has marked ideas of just what "the right girl" would be like. "She's gotta be superfly, nice. She's gotta definitely be built and stacked from the front to the back. I gotta meet her somewhere where she don't know who I am and none of that. She don't know I have a record or anything like that, I want to meet someone who doesn't know who I am, who just likes me for me."

He may not have found that person yet, but Marky hasn't been wholly un-successful in relationships. According to reports, he "quietly romanced" singer Martika for a while. And he does have a special bond to 15-year-old actress Soleil Moon Frye, best remembered as TV's Punky Brewster. Soleil, who ad-mitted to a major crush on Mark, became quite a close friend—"best buds," as she termed it.

Marky has said over and over again that he wants his listeners to pay attention to his lyrics. Those who do, however, have come up with other theories about why Marky may not be ready for true love. Women are routinely dissed in rap lyrics, referred to in highly insulting terms. While most of Mark's raps are pretty neutral, there are a few that do trash women, especially in the song "I Need Money." Marky is rarely called on it, but once when he *was*, he insisted he was only joking, that he didn't really mean it.

He wasn't joking, however, on another occasion. This happened on television in Britain. Eyewitnesses report that on camera, Marky tried to grab the chest of the woman, Amanda de Cadenet, who was interviewing him. He *was* called on it. In his defense he said, "She felt *my* breasts. She's got nice big breasts. I'd love to feel them. I'd love to suck them. There's nothing wrong with that, shit! She's a woman, I'm a man. She has big titties and I'd love to suck them if I had

◉◉◉◉◉◉◉

Soleil Moon Frye is a friend, but when he meets the right girl, "I'm gonna kick her so much rap, she won't know what happened!"

the chance. I'd love to do lots of things to her—what's wrong with that? That's not bad. What's so dirty about feeling someone's breasts? It's like, you don't think girls *want* me to feel their breasts? People made a big deal out of me grabbing her breasts—why? She said to me, 'I heard you have a very big chest.' And I said, 'I heard *you* have a very big chest too. And as a matter of fact, I think yours is a little bigger than mine.' And she said, 'Why don't we find out?' And I said, 'Great, I'm glad you asked me, before I was gonna ask you.' But you

(Janet Macoska)

Who says fans don't get to meet Marky backstage? The Jammin' 92 contest winners in Cleveland get the pic of a lifetime.

see, she was pregnant, so I did not want to get too deep into it—but she wanted to measure my chest."

Perhaps, after all, Marky has a long way to go and a lot to learn about women, relationships, and love. He's only 21 years old, however, and time is on his side.

15

Brotherly Love

Like all long-lasting relationships, the one between Donnie and Mark Wahlberg has evolved considerably over the years. When they were kids, Donnie was the older, smarter, tougher one who looked out for Mark, the baby who needed guidance and protection. As they became young men, and Donnie embarked on a new life, they drifted apart. Donnie was livin' large; Mark was livin' on the edge. But the split proved temporary, as Donnie eventually resumed his place in Mark's life, this time as mentor to a very eager, but raw student. Donnie taught Mark how to turn his rough raps into music and put a group together. In getting behind the controls himself producing Mark's record, Donnie Wahlberg made Marky Mark and the Funky Bunch happen. He gave his brother a career, and a new life. Mark learned his lessons well. He took the ball, ran with it, and scored the ultimate touchdown.

It may seem that Donnie has always been the giver in this relationship, and Mark the taker. But that would be missing the—ahem—mark. For as much as Donnie gave, Mark gave *him* something even more powerful: the chance to express a long-suppressed side of himself. Marky Mark became the conduit through which Donnie was able to return to his own rap roots, something he could never do with New Kids. As Marky himself put it, "Donnie's always been a rapper at heart, but he's just turning to it now. That's okay with the New Kids *now*—it wouldn't have been before. Then, it would have been like putting one of Motley Crue into the Beatles. It's just two totally different things. It wouldn't have worked."

Marky, of course, was the up-front person in Marky Mark and the Funky Bunch, but it was Donnie who pulled the strings, manipulated the image, the sound, the vision, *and* the message. As the driving force behind Marky Mark and the Funky Bunch, Donnie got something else out of the deal. He gained respect as a music producer and as someone who can get a project off the ground and moving up the charts. No easy feat, even for a music veteran. Marky Mark and the Funky Bunch gave Donnie the key to his own future, for certainly that success helped him land the production deal he now has at Interscope Records.

Personally, the relationship between Donnie and Mark has never been better, although they did go though a couple of rocky patches when they first began working together. It wasn't always easy for Mark to accept his big brother as, in effect, his boss. And Donnie proved a tough taskmaster. Mark, who admits that he used to have a tendency to be lazy about his work, reveals, "When we first began working together on *Music for the People*, I didn't like Donnie pressuring me. But I slowly began to see how hard *he* works. He didn't think he was pushing me. He's just a perfectionist and had high expectations of me. Eventually I realized that I really did have to give 100 percent all the time, so I stopped feeling like, 'Hey, take it easy on me!'"

Perhaps even more importantly, Mark came to understand how much Donnie had matured. "We've both always been pretty wild," he says, "but my brother can also be very levelheaded. Like, everyone likes havin' fun, but when it comes down to it, you know, he is the first one to cut out the jokin' and get down to business. It took a while to learn that I had to look at him differently than I did when I was younger."

It's only recently that Mark has come to fully appreciate the value of the advice he has gotten from his older brother. "Because he went through and dealt with a lot of things, that saved me a lot of headaches. Because he sometimes made the wrong decision, I was able to avoid them. He gave me lots of basic advice, just to stay levelheaded and don't get caught by hype and all the fame, to stay focused and concentrate." And Marky adds this bit of even more telling "insider" advice: "He taught me to always let somebody else take the blame, don't be the bad guy. Let the record company be the bad guy."

For his part, Donnie too has come to see different sides of his brother. Donnie's divulged, "Mark is very caring, but he is also quite 'street' and hip about things. He is really funny and his sense of humor makes his music all the better. It

"I've been learning a lot from Donnie, he's a great producer."

(John Barrett)

"It's cool when Donnie's home. I guess
I do miss him when he's away.
Sometimes. Not all the time."

amazes me to see how Marky takes control of a stage...once he gets onstage, he dominates it! I'm really happy I could help him get what I already have. That's more important to me than other things, like my own career. Now I'm really proud of him. He's my brother *and* he's nice."

It hasn't only been career advice that Mark has gotten from Donnie, as he reveals: "I guess the best advice I've had in life has been from him. He told me never to forget who I was, no matter what happened to me, or what I became in life. I'll remember that always."

Their relationship continues to evolve. Increasingly, Donnie and Marky see themselves as equals. Both agree that Marky is ready to take more creative control on his next CD.

16

"This Is How I Am"

Just as Marky's relationship with Donnie has evolved over the years, so that once-brash young boy is slowly changing into a mellower, more introspective young man. He understands that life is a series of choices, and that for many years he insisted on making the wrong ones. Marky's making new choices now. The onetime "proud to be a street kid" now sees himself as "street survivor."

That said, however, there's little danger of Marky turning into a super-straight, totally reformed, buttoned-down drudge. Marky could never be that one-dimensional. Just like on his CD, there are two distinct sides to Marky, the "Wild Side" and the "Smoove Side." Details Marky, "I can be wild, but like my record, I'm very versatile. I can be outspoken at times, and I can be very quiet at others, and just analyze situations. Like I'm wild on stage—I just let it all go."

No kidding. Marky's wild side *is* on overdrive on stage. Between his angry rap scowl and titillating lyrical and sexual antics, no one's yet confused him with, say, Michael Bolton. Off stage, it's Marky's "major attitude" that saves his rap-scallion reputation. Upholding a proud tradition of rappers, he is boastful and *mouthy*. According to at least one journalist, Marky "swears more than any other human being alive. He talks constantly—about anything that comes to mind: muscles, food, his rise to fame, his friends, cars, girls...more girls. There is not a single sentence that doesn't include a four-letter word. And when he's not talking, he's making up risqué raps all the time."

Marky makes no apologies for his mouth. "I *like* being outrageous," he asserts. "If I think it's necessary to speak about something then I will definitely go out of my way to say it. I think my opinion is cool and I got a chance to voice it . . . so I tell the truth about how I feel."

Mark claims to one-up his brother, even, in street swagger. "I have a worse attitude than Donnie," he bragged to a reporter. "It's just like 'Don't mess with us,' know what I'm saying'? We don't like to be messed with."

"As a singer, you have a big effect on people. I felt ready to make a half-decent effect on other people's lives."

ⓄⓄⓄⓄⓄⓄⓄ

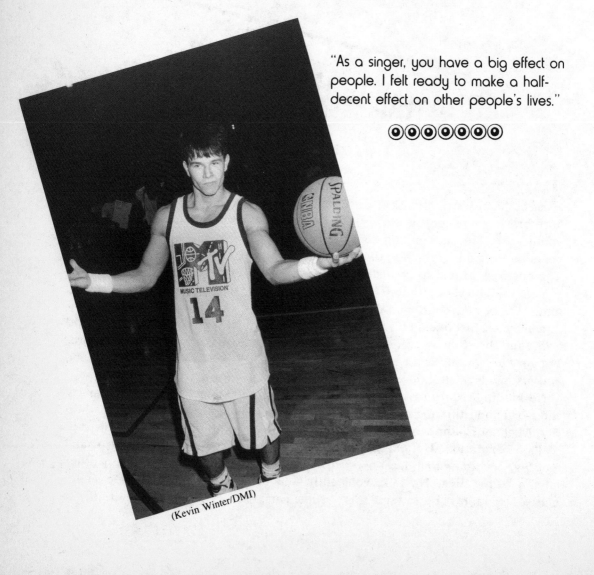

(Kevin Winter/DMI)

Much as he's proud of his tough veneer, Marky stops short at suggestions that he was ever a really bad kid. Where he came from, "bad" meant you had more than misdemeanors on your record. "I am not a bad kid," Marky said. "If you see me or Donnie as bad, you must have grown up in some little bullshit town [that] when somebody spit on the sidewalk, it's like headline news. To be considered a bad person where *I* came from, you'd better be shooting and killing people!" It's, like, all relative.

He further breaks it down: "Okay, so I did quit high school at quite a young age, but a bad person would not be trying to go back and better himself like I'm doing. I'm trying to make a positive turn in my life... which I was doing before I had a record out."

Which actually happens to be true. Marky *has* made some changes in his life. Before he became a star, he did, in fact, start studying for his GED—general equivalency diploma—which, once passed, will make Marky a high-school graduate. He began studying in 1990, when he was at the Dorchester Youth Collaborative. There, in trying to turn his life around, he realized that "I missed out on a lot of things—my prom, my graduation. I don't want to make any more mistakes like that." He started by taking courses at night school, which he found "real easy, basic stuff." It got harder. Like the time Marky—following in the frustrated footsteps of so many students before him—once exploded over the periodic table of the elements. "I just got a science book—science is the worst, man! Sometimes when I'm stuck on the bus, studying a science book, I say, 'I could have been done with this three years ago, if I wasn't such a lazy hardheaded... You know what I'm saying.'" Still, Marky plugs on with the books. He has come to realize that "It's very important to me. It's good that I want to go back to school. I realize that it's important that I want to do these things. They are more steps in the right direction."

Another of those steps: Marky, under the guidance and tutelage of his beloved parish priest, Father Flavin, was recently confirmed in the Catholic Church. "My mother always wanted us to go to church on Sundays," he muses, "and because of that, Father Flavin has become a close friend. God has just been a big part of my life. I've seen that. I just feel that the spiritual side of life is important. It helps you become a better person."

Because of the celebrity weight he now carries, Marky has the chance to do good for others—and he's not wasted an opportunity. Raising AIDS awareness and funds for research is the cause Marky feels most strongly about. He participated in Planet Hollywood's "Kiss AIDS Goodbye" benefit as well as the TJ Martell Foundation's Rock 'N' Jock basketball game. Proceeds from that all-star

Along with Luke Perry from "Beverly Hills, 90210," Marky played for keeps in the MTV Rock 'N' Jock basketball game to benefit the Pediatric AIDS Foundation.

event (at which Marky not only shot hoops, but performed as well) went to the Pediatric AIDS Foundation.

Indeed, one of the choices he *has* made lately is not only to better himself, but to be a role model of sorts, and especially for kids who grow up without many advantages. Marky well understands what he represents to those kids. "I know a lot of people who look at me doing positive things with my life...that my actions and my music have been positive. To have that impact on someone's

He appeared at Planet Hollywood's "Kiss AIDS Goodbye" fund-raiser as well.

(Albert Ferreira/DMI)

life is a great feeling. I'm not fakin' it, I *am* a positive person, and if I can give a positive outlook to people, who, like me, grew up without many opportunities, then that's a great accomplishment. It's amazing how good you can feel about yourself when you're doing good things."

17

Forging Ahead

Marky's a man with a plan. Though firmly settled on the hype tip, there's no way he's about to stay put, musically *or* personally. Marky is moving on, with a vengeance and a vision. A year ago, he said he just wanted "to go on making good records, write raps with meaning... and have a good time while I'm doing it." Now, he sees things in a little more detail. He's taken the time to reflect on how he got so far, so fast—and he's decided exactly where he wants to go from here.

First up on the agenda is a musical mission: album number two, or, as he calls it, "Project '92: You Gotta Believe." Don't expect a carbon copy of *Music for the People*. "I'm coming out totally different on the next album," Marky hints. He doesn't mean that he'll abandon the kinds of hip-hop tunes that made him famous. No one will confuse Mark's next album with Harry Connick, Jr.'s. But now that he's got the "popular vote," this boy wants respect, from the music industry and from the critics. To that end, he hints of tuning down the titillation meter by a few megawatts. "That's not what I want to be remembered for," he told a reporter for the *New York Times*. "People loved it—wow, this kid's running around on TV in his underwear! But now that I got them interested, I want to make a good [musical] impression."

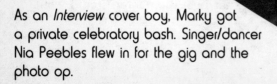

"Half-wild, half-child" was the name of the story in *Interview*. Marky takes the hype tip only half-seriously.

(Albert Ferreira/DMI)

(Albert Ferreira/DMI)

As an *Interview* cover boy, Marky got a private celebratory bash. Singer/dancer Nia Peebles flew in for the gig and the photo op.

Uh-oh. Does that mean...gulp...no more shirtless shenanigans? No more low-riding briefs and stripteases? Well, not exactly. Marky assures his audience, "I'll still work out, and I'll still take off my shirt and stuff. Then again, I'm not going to go out there and just flaunt it."

The wait for the "new" Marky—on album *and* on stage— won't be a long one, for he is at work right now on his sophomore effort, due out before the close of 1992. Along with it, Marky will, of course, tour. Backed by the Funky Bunch, this time he'll play bigger venues on a more extensive itinerary. Europe, Japan, and Australia are on the docket this time around.

Beyond that, might Marky make a rap record with Donnie up front? It's been discussed, but it's doubtful. Donnie might lay down a guest rap or two on the new album, but there are no plans just yet for a Wahlberg brothers CD.

The question comes up more in the European press than in the United States, but still it is asked with frequency: any chance of Marky rejoining NKOTB? His answer: "No! If I'd wanted to be a member of the New Kids, I would not have left them way back. They are still not a rap group...and even if they were, I'm doing my own thing now. I can't see me and Jordan Knight rapping together!"

Can he see himself branching out into other kinds of entertainment? It's been suggested, more than once, that Marky might make a major movie star. Film studios have, in fact, extended offers, but Marky's not making any moves in that direction just yet. In a few years, though, who knows?

In the meantime, the merchandising of Marky paraphernalia steamrolls ahead. Right now, fans can buy T-shirts, jackets, posters, buttons, and backstage-pass icons, all emblazoned with Marky's logo. His line of underwear—boxer shorts— is the best seller by far. Small wonder.

There's more on Marky's mind, however, than just the show-biz stuff. In quiet moments, when he looks ahead, he realizes full well that all the glitz will someday fade to black. Much as he feels there will always be a place for him in the music world, Marky has his sights set on something he *never* would have imagined just a few years back: a college education. As he recently admitted, "Hopefully, I can go to college and do something afterward—as much as I love what I'm doing, I don't feel it will last forever." Spoken with a newly gained maturity from a young man who has learned a great deal over the past two years, one who is emerging with a voice and a vision all his own.

Marky used to say his ultimate goal was success. But now, he simply says it is "Peace."

Pretty-boy movie star Richard Grieco signed a deal to direct films. Would Marky make a movie star? Could be.

(Albert Ferreira/DMI)

18

Facts on File

Real full name: Mark Robert Michael Wahlberg.

Nicknames: Monk D. (from Donnie), Monk Dilla, Marky Mark.

Birthday: June 5, 1971.

Born and raised in: Boston, Massachusetts.

Height, weight: 5'9" tall, 150 pounds.

Hair, eyes: Brown hair. His hazel eyes "come from my father. They change, depending my on mood. Mostly they're brown, but sometimes they're green."

Family: Alma and Donald are his natural parents; Mark Conroy is his stepdad. Tracey, Michelle, and Debbie are his older sisters; Arthur, Paul, Bob, Jim, and Donnie are the big brothers. Brandon and Adam are Mark's nephews.

Lives now: In a large, modern home with a basketball court and swimming pool in the Boston suburb of Braintree.

School: Marky dropped out of high school, but will graduate with a GED soon.

Drives: A black Jeep Cherokee and a brand new Mercedes.

Favorites:

  Music: Rap, soul, reggae, house music.

  Food: Turkey, chicken, vegetables, fruit—with an occasional McDonald's and/ or Snickers lapse.

Drink: Health-food concoction, with protein powder and pineapple juice—with an occasional Pepsi lapse.

Color: Black

Sports: Basketball, football, foozball, baseball.

Team: Boston Celtics (basketball).

Ultimate Goal: "Peace."

Best addresses: Interscope Records, 10900 Wilshire Boulevard, Suite 1400, Los Angeles, CA 90024; or Dick Scott Management, 888 Seventh Avenue, New York, NY 10019; or Marky Mark and the Funky Bunch Fan Club, P.O. Box 207, Quincy, MA 02269.

Discography/Videography

CD: *Marky Mark and The Funky Bunch, Music for the People*/Interscope Records, 1991.

Tracks: "Music for the People"; "Good Vibrations"; "Wildside"; "'Bout Time I Funk You"; "Peace"; "So What Chu Sayin'"; "Marky Mark Is Here"; "On the House Tip"; "Make Me Say Ooh!"; "I Need Money"; "The Last Song on Side B."

Singles: *"Good Vibrations"; "Wildside"; "I Need Money"; "Peace."*

Long-form video: Marky Mark and The Funky Bunch, Music for the People, 1992 release.

Clips: "Good Vibrations"; "Wildside"; "I Need Money"; plus live European and U.S. tour performances, interviews, behind the scenes/A*Vision Entertainment/60 minutes.

About the Author

Randi Reisfeld has been chronicling the pop culture scene for many years. In her position as editorial director of *16* magazine she has interviewed and written about the careers of the hottest musical and TV/movie personalities of the past decade.

She has written a host of popular biographies, among them *Johnny Depp*; *Debbie Gibson: Electric Star*; *Nelson: Double Play*; *The Stars of Beverly Hills, 90210: Their Lives and Loves*; *Loving Luke: The Luke Perry Story*; *Young Stars, featuring Macaulay Culkin*; and collaborated with Vanilla Ice on *Ice By Ice* (Avon Books).

Additionally, she has written the definitive how-to guide for young show-biz hopefuls: *So You Want to Be a Star!: The Teenager's Guide to Breaking into Showbiz*.

Ms. Reisfeld's work has also appeared in The *New York Times*, *Scholastic*, *Welsh publications*, and *Woman's World*.

She lives in the New York area with her husband and teenage children amid the constant blare of rap music, especially that by Marky Mark and the Funky Bunch!